Lead Deeper

Advance Praise for
Lead Deeper

"Rondi Pogue is a Spirit-filled, Jesus-loving author and speaker who has created an incredible tool for teachers, youth workers, mentors, and parents. Our current culture sends a lot of unhealthy mixed messages to our young women, and this book provides Biblical leading so that our girls can live a life of freedom. *Lead Deeper* is filled with transformative truths that will help our young women dig into and discover the lies they may be believing about themselves and replace those lies with the truth of who God made them to be."

~ Kristi Ellis, Professor & Vice Principle

"In *Lead Deeper*, Rondi takes us on a beautiful journey of teaching leaders who lead young women how to allow the ministry we do to be an overflow of the transformative work the Lord has first done in our own lives. In a generation of girls who are dealing with eating disorders, abuse, trauma, depression, mental illness, suicide, and broken homes, the question of "How do we help these girls?" can often overwhelm our thoughts and cripple our ministry. This book is a beautiful representation of the Lord handing you a sword and teaching you how to do battle with and for the young women in your world. For you to feel equipped, empowered, confident, and able to do the work the Lord has called you to, Rondi Pogue is not only a pioneer in the how-tos of reaching young women, but her life has impacted young women around the world including myself. This book is for such a time as this and an answer to help a generation of girls who are hurting, feeling hopeless and lost."

~ **Christina Bourdreau, Plus Size Model, Author, Speaker, and Whosoevers Ambassador**

"I have rarely encountered voices that speak to the cultural lies binding today's women like Rondi Pogue. Having witnessed her powerful personal transformation firsthand I can attest that Rondi is the real deal and a hard-hitting author who is passionate to help women unveil the lies that bind them! If you want freedom, this is the author for you."

~ **Adam Stadtmiller, Author of *Praying For Your Elephant* David C. Cook & Pastor**

"Rondi Pogue has distilled years of ministry experience with young women into this timely, powerful book. This is an asset for anyone working with students to help them uncover the lies that have shaped their thinking and embrace the truth of their identity in Christ. Now, more than ever, we need these tools to equip the next generation."

~ **Mark Foreman, Author & Pastor**

"Our culture is telling young women lies about who they are and what determines their worth. Rondi Pogue has a heart for God and His truth and a passion to see the lives of young women changed through the unveiling of these lies. This must-read book is a playbook to combat those lies and help young women cling to the truth of who they are in Christ so that they can experience a life of freedom in Jesus."

~ Colin Sinclair, So Cal FCA Director

"All matter of opinions exist regarding solutions to the lack of value, significance, and worth felt by women in our nation and worldwide. While most are painting broad strokes with little depth, Rondi has spent her time in pursuit of Christ and the women He loves to discover the root. From the shores of SoCal to the villages of India to the cells of women's prisons, what God has confirmed through Rondi and Unveiling is the power of His Truth to set women free. This book is a much-needed, practical guide out of the forest of lies women believe and into the Truth their souls were made for."

~ Lynsey Dietze, Director of Women Engaging

Lead Deeper

EQUIPPING YOU TO EMPOWER
THE YOUNG WOMEN YOU LEAD

Rondi Pogue

NEW YORK

LONDON • NASHVILLE • MELBOURNE • VANCOUVER

Lead Deeper

Equipping You to Empower the Young Women You Lead

© 2021 Rondi Pogue

Published in New York, New York, by Morgan James Publishing. Morgan James is a trademark of Morgan James, LLC. www.MorganJamesPublishing.com

ISBN 9781631952661 paperback
ISBN 9781631952678 eBook
Library of Congress Control Number: 2020940771

Cover Design by:
Rachel Lopez
www.r2cdesign.com

Interior Design by:
Chris Treccani
www.3dogcreative.net

Morgan James is a proud partner of Habitat for Humanity Peninsula and Greater Williamsburg. Partners in building since 2006.

Get involved today! Visit
MorganJamesPublishing.com/giving-back

This book is dedicated to all females who work with young women. You have one of the hardest, most thankless, yet most important and fun jobs. Your role in young women's lives is so crucial—never believe the lies that tell you otherwise. You are seen. You are appreciated. You are deeply loved.

UNVEILING'S MISSION

"To empower young women by providing help, tools, and encouragement to those who work with young women because pouring into today's youth is one of the most important roles!"

TABLE OF CONTENTS

Foreword

I have a hunch that you really like to read. I know this for two reasons: Reason #1, you are reading this book; Reason #2, you are reading the Foreword to this book and only people who really like to read take time to read the Foreword of a book! I like to read, too, and I especially like to read books written by folks who are both knowledgeable and passionate about their topic. Lots of people are passionate, but don't have knowledge, and lots of people have loads of knowledge but have lost some passion along the way. So, when I find somebody with knowledge and passion … I read what they write! My friend Rondi Pogue is one such person.

I've known Rondi for years and have watched both up close and from a distance as she has grown as a follower of Jesus, a leader, a youth pastor, a ministry leader, and a movement starter. When it comes to leading and pastoring young women, few people have more knowledge and experience than Rondi. And when it comes to helping them discover and live out their identity in Christ, few people have more passion. Rondi has dedicated her life to helping young women understand and live into their identity in Christ. It's in her DNA. It leaks out of her. She can't not talk about it. She couldn't not write about it!

In your hands you are holding a labor of love birthed out of Rondi's personal journey, her experience as a youth pastor, and her never-ending quest to help young women, and the leaders who work with them, experience the true fullness of life found only in Jesus. I like to remind folks all the time that powerful things often come in small packages (probably because I'm only 5'8"). This is a small, but very powerful, book. There are no wasted words and no "filler" stories included just to meet the publisher's word count. It won't take you long to read, but it will have a long-lasting impact in your ministry to young women. When you read a book about ministry, it typically ends up falling into one of two camps: books you read for education and books you read for implementation. I hope for you *Lead Deeper* falls into the latter category. I hope you learn a thing or two, but my bigger hope is that you will prayerfully seek how you might begin to implement some of what you learn into your ministry setting.

The young women in your ministry are one-of-a-kind, handcrafted masterpieces. They bear the image of God himself! Sadly, they live in a world that is constantly chipping away at their ability to fully embrace their amazing identity. All of us who work with young women know this to be true and many of us have struggled in our efforts to help. In this book, help has arrived, and I'm so thankful Rondi has put her knowledge and passion into this book and made it available to the rest of us!

Kurt Johnston
Pastor of NextGen Ministries; Saddleback Church
Twitter: @kurtjohnston Insta: Kurtjohnston

Chapter 1:

Difference Maker

Life is hard, and it comes at us fast! I think most of us begin to realize this after college, but I'm noticing more and more high school students learning this early on. High school students are transitioning from a state of innocence to a greater understanding of reality and responsibility earlier than most of us did. They are beginning to develop an awareness of what is really going on around them. New feelings are starting to arise, and they are questioning themselves in new ways. That is why working with youth is so important.

Here is one of the great things about youth: They tend to be more open, more teachable, and definitely more moldable than adults. And while they may look a lot like adults, emotionally and cognitively, they are not. The older we get, the less we want to deal with our hurts and struggles because their presence has created deep pain. Youth, on the other hand, haven't had the years to allow the hurts to sink deep and grow. They still tend to have childlike faith, and their "soil" is soft, making them open to change, healing, and correction. That's why working with youth can be so exciting—typically, they are willing to enter into the messy parts of life and do the hard work.

Young women need help and guidance from adults who truly care about them. Far too often, few people are pouring into their lives emotionally. And the adults who are "supposed to" do this (specifically, their parents) are not the ones teenagers want to hear from. I have worked with youth since 2002, and as each year goes by, it's become more and more apparent how important it is for students to have youth pastors, mentors, youth volunteers, and youth leaders in their lives. As the book *Sticky Faith* discovered,[1] "Each young person is greatly benefited when surrounded by a team of five adults. We call this the new 5:1 ratio." They found that students are more likely to

---

1   *Sticky Faith* by Chap Clark and Kara E. Powell

keep living out their faith and make wise decisions when they have five adults pouring into their lives. You play a significant role in these students' lives because of your investment in them.

Working with youth can be incredibly tiring while also being so much fun! It can sometimes be a thankless job, and we often wonder if teenagers are even listening. So, before we continue, let me say this: THANK YOU! Thank you for the time, energy, resources, and love you give to today's youth. God is using you—please hear that loud and clear! I have countless stories of students coming to me years later and telling me how what I taught on a Sunday morning or a trip or a one-on-one conversation that I don't even remember has impacted their lives.

Just the other day, I was at the gym, and I ran into a woman whose sons were in my youth group five years prior. She and I caught up on life and then went on our ways. Later that week, I ran into her again, and she said, "I told my sons that I saw you and they totally remembered you. One of them said, 'I remember one Sunday she taught on comparison!'" I can't tell you what someone else spoke on five years ago, let alone what I spoke on five years ago—so how did he remember? I was on a high for the next week because I was so encouraged to hear how God had used me. I had no idea that talk impacted someone's life, and at least one person still remembered it years later.

I know we don't do the work solely to see the fruit of our labor. We do the work because God has called us to do it and we want to be obedient. But I pray that God allows you to see the fruit of your labor. Seeing the fruit of my labor has encouraged me and helped me to press in and press on, especially during seasons of exhaustion and discouragement.

This is a book I wish I could've read when I worked in full-time youth ministry. I didn't have the time or energy to sit down and read an average-size book. I wanted a practical book that I could quickly read, relate to, and use as a tool for the girls I worked with. My hope and prayer is that this book will enable and empower you so you can enable and empower your students to move beyond their surface issues and deal with the root causes. This is the only way to truly help them with the problems they face. I'm sure your heart is the same as mine: We want to help young women learn how to fight the battles and lies they face and truly live in freedom!

Chapter 1 Summary

Well done, my fellow youth workers! God is
using you to make a difference!

Chapter 2:

Dig It Up

I'm a pretty easygoing person, and I try not to let stuff bother me. "You have to pick and choose your battles" is one of my life mottos, and I don't choose many battles because I don't have the time or energy to confront everything and everyone that hurts my feelings.

A while ago, I was planning a birthday party for a friend (let's call her Jill) when she called and told me that she didn't want to have a party anymore. She explained that life was too crazy and she was getting stressed out. I wasn't upset at all because I understood where she was coming from—I might have even done the same thing given the circumstances.

Two days later, a mutual friend sent out an email to Jill's closest friends announcing a mini birthday breakfast celebration for Jill. The email confused me because I had just talked to Jill two days earlier and she made it very clear that she didn't want to do anything for her birthday this year! I called Jill to see if she was okay with this birthday breakfast and she said, "Yes, she called me and asked if a small celebration with my close friends over breakfast would be okay and I agreed to it." I was furious. I was hurt. My usual response to a glitch like this was to be disappointed and then quickly get over it. This time I was outraged—I didn't even want to talk to Jill anymore.

I remember thinking to myself, "Why am I so outraged? Why am I allowing something so small to bother me so much?" I prayed and asked God to show me what was going on because I suspected that the surface issue was not the true issue. There was something else going on and I needed to figure it out. Over the next week, God started to show me that the reason I was so hurt was that I felt left out. Left out of helping to plan the birthday celebration. I didn't feel included; instead, I felt like an outsider.

As I sat and processed the whole turn of events with the Lord, I realized that I was so hurt and outraged because I had been feeling really lonely. At thirty-seven years old and single, I live alone and work from home alone. Life is naturally lonely for me. I also often feel left out because most of my friends are married and have kids, and they lead incredibly busy lives with their families. When they do have free time, they want to hang out with their married friends and their friends with children. They aren't intentionally leaving me out or telling me I'm not welcome, but, nonetheless, I sometimes still feel left out and alone—like an outsider. As I thought things through, it made sense why something so small led me to react with such intense outrage and hurt.

Once God showed me the root issue, I was able to work it out with Him, talk to Jill, and ask her forgiveness for pushing her away and being bitter. Then we were able to put the whole thing behind us and move on.

I want to share another story with you about digging deeper and finding the root of our problems and how helpful it can be. One year ago, I was going to a bunch of weddings and events in a very short period (there were almost two events a week for a month). Since I'm single, I didn't have a date to go with, and I wasn't even sure if I would know anyone at the events. I'm used to going to things alone because when you are single at thirty-seven years old, that's what happens. I prefer to go with someone, but that's just not my reality right now. At the end of that busy month, I felt very defeated and frustrated. Not about the fact that I was alone or single, but because as I looked back over the month, I binged before or after every event I went to. I called my mentor and asked to meet so we could talk through it. We met and were both stumped about why I was binge eating so much that month. We decided I should go to seeing my therapist for several sessions to figure out what was going on and how to deal with it.

After only one session, my therapist helped me figure out that I was binge eating before events because I was afraid of not connecting with someone at the event since I was going alone. I would "connect" with food and numb myself in case I didn't end up connecting with someone when I arrived. The times I would binge eat after the event were because I didn't connect with anyone, so I would come home and "connect" with food and numb myself because of the pain I was feeling: lonely, left out, not connected, not loved.

Mind. Blown. Not only did the last month make sense, but looking back, my whole life made sense. There were times when I was younger that I would binge eat, and I never knew why. Now, all of a sudden, I saw why I did what I did. I am a one-on-one connector. I do not like big groups; I prefer hanging out with just one other person. When I don't get to really connect with someone, I start hearing lies about who I am. The lies creep in and tell me I am unwanted, unloved, undesired, weird or I have a horrible personality—and the list goes on. Connecting with others gives me life and energy and makes me feel loved, known, seen, and wanted.

Knowing why I did what I did was helpful and freeing. It lifted the frustrations and heaviness and gave me hope. Now that I know the problem, I can work toward a solution and stop it from happening again. I continued to meet with my therapist for two more months, which allowed me to dig deeper and learn healthy ways to cope.

I have been going to therapy for over twelve years, and it has been very helpful. Sometimes you need an outside perspective and someone who isn't emotionally involved in the hurts and struggles of your life. Years ago, while in a therapy session, my counselor said something I found very profound: **"If something is hysterical, that means it is historical."** In other words, if I react to something hysterically (with an immediate, overwhelmingly emotional response—like I did with Jill), that response traces back to something historical that happened in my life. The current issue is not the only issue; there is a deeper underlying cause.

We have all had experiences when students talk to us about their problems (sometimes petty teenager issues) and we sit back and wonder why something so insignificant is having such an overwhelming effect on them. Our initial reaction is to kindly tell them to get over it and move on. But that approach does nothing to address the deeper issue. We need to help them discover the deeper issue so they can heal the wound and move forward.

If we just address the surface issue with the students and don't help them get to the root of the problem, we are doing them a great disservice. Just like a weed, if the root isn't pulled up and removed from the soil, the issue will keep popping up, forcing them (and you) to deal with it again and again.

I want to help young people as much as I can while they are young so when they enter adulthood, they will be better able to handle life's challenges. I believe part of our calling and mission is to help them discover why they think what they think and why they do what they do. This will enable them to see old wounds heal and change their unhealthy coping habits.

Not too long ago, I was getting irritated with people very quickly. And when I say people, I mean everyone—yes, everyone was annoying me. I would complain about them in my head after I talked to them, and I even rolled my eyes behind their back as I walked away. Essentially, everyone was bothering me all the time. If you know me, you know this isn't my norm. One day while I was driving, the Holy Spirit gently whispered to me, "We don't do things for no reason." My eyes got big and my stomach dropped because I knew what God was telling me at that moment. I was pointing the finger at everyone else because they were the issue, but I knew He was showing me that my frustrations were stemming from something within ME. I had a deep gut feeling that it had nothing to do with others. It was time to stop and take inventory of my life and heart and do the hard work of digging deeper.

We are not trying to be counselors or therapists; we are looking to God and asking Him for wisdom, discernment, and insight so we can guide each student to health, healing, and God. We need to ask Him to help us see what they cannot see—and sometimes what we cannot see—so we can help them as they grow into healthy adults. It is best to help our students discover their root issues on their own instead of telling them what we think those issues might be.

With that being said, there might come a time where you think the young woman you are meeting with needs more help than you can give, and that's okay! There are times when past pains and circumstances are so deep that it takes a trained professional to best help someone. Kindly and gently suggest they see a therapist, and if you know of any good therapists, recommend them to someone who you know and trust. I saw a therapist for many years, and I still go on and off as needed. Counseling is not a sign of weakness; seeing a therapist is a sign of strength.

So how do we help them find the root issue to their problems? Ask questions. Then keep asking questions. This is something we see modeled in Scripture.

- *"But the Lord God called to the man, 'Where are you?'" (Genesis 3:9 NIV)*
- *"Who of you by worrying can add a single hour to his life?" (Matthew 6:27 BSB)*
- *"Do you believe that I am able to do this?" (Matthew 9:28 NIV)*
- *"Who do you say I am?" (Matthew 16:15 NIV)*
- *"What do you think? If a man owns a hundred sheep, and one of them wanders away, will he not leave the*

ninety-nine on the hills and go to look for the one that wandered off?" (Matthew 18:12 NIV)

- *"Do you now believe? Jesus replied." (John 16:31 NIV)*

- *"Here a great number of disabled people used to lie— the blind, the lame, the paralyzed. One who was there had been an invalid for thirty-eight years. When Jesus saw him lying there and learned that he had been in this condition for a long time, he asked him, 'Do you want to get well?'" (John 5:3-6 NIV)*

- *"He replied, 'You of little faith, why are you so afraid?'" (Matthew 8:26 NIV)*

- *"Jesus answered, 'What is written in the Scriptures? How do you understand them?'" (Luke 10:26 CEV)*

- *"When Jesus and his disciples had finished eating, he asked, 'Simon son of John, do you love me more than the others do?'" (John 21:15 CEV)*

These questions were tailored to help individual people discover the issues beneath their behavior. Without this understanding, there can be no healing.

There was a question someone very special in my life asked me over twelve years ago, and that question has changed my life. At the time the question was asked, I was the High School Director at a church, and I was in a serious relationship. I had just finished working for the day, so I headed to the parking lot to get in my car to go home, and as I was walking across the parking lot, I ran into another pastor I worked with. He asked me how I was doing. I proceeded to tell him that life was good, ministry was well, but I was struggling in my dating relationship.

The relationship I was in was very serious, and we had just started talking about engagement. I was looking at rings. But I was having some doubts. I opened up and shared this with the pastor. He was very kind, and he just listened to me pour out the confusion I was feeling in my heart. Once I was finished sharing with him, he looked at me and said, "I am going to ask you a question, but I do not want you to give me your answer. You could marry Mark (name changed for protection), and it could be a good marriage, it could even be a great marriage, but would it be God's best marriage for you?" He then walked away.

As I slowly walked to my car, thinking through what he had just asked me, I knew the answer to his question. I don't want good. I don't want great. I only want God's best, and this relationship wasn't His best for me. It didn't mean Mark was a bad guy; it just meant He wasn't God's best for me, and I knew the hard conversation I now needed to have with Mark.

You see, one question can change a person's life, and I think if the pastor I ran into told me that Mark wasn't God's best for me, I probably wouldn't have listened. Most likely, I would have gotten defensive. But this pastor allowed me to think through it for myself, and he let the Holy Spirit do the work in me and lead my heart to where God's heart was.

That question was life-changing for me. Questions are one of the simplest and most effective ways of learning. It helps us gain more in-depth insight, and that is why Jesus asked so many questions.

Recently I met up with a previous student of mine who is now in the workforce. She shared that she had been struggling with not feeling beautiful. I had no idea what could be at the root of this struggle. So, I started respectfully probing by asking questions. "When do you tend to not feel beautiful? Is it when you are around certain people, on Instagram, around family, or some other setting?"

She told me she usually feels that way when she turns to food out of stress and doesn't work out.

I then asked, "What do you tend to do to 'fix' not feeling beautiful? Do you put on more makeup, change your hair, buy new clothes, or do something else?"

She quickly responded, "No, I go work out."

I then asked, "How does working out correlate with beauty to you?"

She sat back in her chair and said, "I don't know. Hmmm." She sat with the question for a couple of minutes and then said, "I was raised in a very healthy household, and we were always active, so being fit is very important to my family."

I said, "Is it part of your family's identity?"

"Yes!" she said.

I then asked, "How do being fit and feeling beautiful go hand in hand to you?"

She was stumped. She took a minute to think through it and said, "Well, I guess being fit doesn't really go hand in hand with beauty, but in my family that is what is valued and considered beautiful. So, when I am not healthy with my food choices and regularly working out, I don't feel beautiful. I don't care about having the right makeup or clothes or hair. I care about my body being in shape." Until this conversation, she had never realized this about her family or herself.

If we had dealt with this issue at just the surface and didn't dig deeper, it might have helped her, and she could have even felt better for a short time, but eventually it would have popped back up because the real issue hadn't been addressed. She and I agreed to talk once a week to help her continue to deal with the root issues. It is such a joy to help her discover the truth of who she really is in Christ and find freedom from the lie that she isn't beautiful.

There is a method I use called **The 5 Whys**. It is easy to remember, simple to use, and helpful when you feel lost and are not sure what questions to ask when you are meeting with young women.

Sakichi Toyoda developed this technique, which basically says, "When a problem occurs, you drill down to its root cause by asking 'why?' five times. The 5 Whys uses 'countermeasures' rather than solutions. A countermeasure is an action or set of actions that seeks to prevent the problem arising again, while a solution may just seek to deal with the symptoms. Because of this, countermeasures are more robust and will more likely prevent the problem from recurring."[2]

---

2   https://www.mindtools.com/pages/article/newTMC_5W.htm

In the image below, you will find an example of how The 5 Whys work. Please note that everyone will answer the whys differently, so the root issue will always be different.

PROBLEM

Girl says she is ugly.

WHY do you feel ugly?
Because I don't have a boyfriend.

WHY does not having a boyfriend make you ugly?
Because no guys like me, so obviously I am not pretty.

WHY do guys date girls... only for their looks?
Well, no. I guess it is more than looks.

WHY is this all of a sudden coming up in your life?
Because a lot of my friends have boyfriends, and I don't.

WHY does it bother you that some friends have a boyfriend?
I'm feeling left out and lonely right now.

ROOT ISSUE

The main issue is not about beauty;
she is feeling lonely and left out.

In my early days of working with youth, I did not feel like I was equipped to serve them well. But God showed me that asking questions is one of the best tools I could use. I may not understand what my students are going through, or even know what to say. But we can all be good listeners and ask questions—you've got this!

Cheers to helping students discover the root cause of a problem. You aren't just helping them at that moment; you are helping them learn skills and tools that will benefit them for a lifetime!

Chapter 2 Summary

Help your students find the root cause to their problem. If we just address the surface issue with the students and don't get to the root of the problem, we are doing girls a great disservice.

Just like a weed, if the root isn't pulled up and removed from the soil, the issue will keep popping up, leaving you and them to deal with it again and again.

Chapter 3:

Identity Theft

Alexandra was a sweet, seventeen-year-old high school junior who sang and danced her way through her teen years. She was happy, motivated, and full of life. Alexandra was recognized for achieving outside the home and was thoroughly cherished inside it.

Just weeks after a family ski vacation, this straight-A student, class officer, and robotics whiz made her bed, tidied her room, and then walked to a highway overpass in Grafton, Massachusetts.

She jumped.

The week after her death, among their daughter's belongings, her parents found two journals filled with

23

phrases and words such as: "I am not good enough. I'm worthless. I am a burden. I am a failure." There were over 200 pages of self-loathing and despair.

I saw this story on *CBS Sunday Morning*, and it gripped my heart. Satan's job is to lie to us, and one of the ways he does this is through our identity. This episode from the *CBS Sunday Morning* show stated that teen suicide is at a forty-year high for young women and is now the second leading cause of death for fifteen- to twenty-four-year-olds of both genders This story reminded me of the importance of making sure our youth know their true identity in Christ.

In Genesis, the snake (Satan) tempted Eve and told her she would be like God if she ate of the fruit. Eve immediately started comparing herself to God, and I believe she experienced an identity crisis for the very first time. This was the first moment when a human didn't feel like she was enough.

Plain and simple, when we don't know our identity in Christ, we struggle in life. Knowing our true identity— who Christ says we are—grounds us and gives us stability. When we don't know who we are in Christ, or we don't believe it, we will make unwise choices rooted in our uncertainty of our value—just like Eve.

We have been struggling with our identity since the beginning of humanity's existence. Satan continues doing the same thing with us that he did with Eve. The Enemy still pulls out all the stops to get us to question our identity as sons and daughters of God. He knows that if he can make us question who we truly are, we will be left adrift to make poor choices that lead us away from God's love and straight to heartbreak and despair.

I believe that everything—yes, *everything*—we struggle with comes down to believing the enemy's lies about our identity. Let's look at the example of Eve again:

- Eve was cursed by God because…
- She ate the fruit because…
- She forgot her true identity and thought she wasn't enough, and she wanted to be like God because…
- She questioned what God told her, and she started comparing herself to God because…
- **Satan lied to her and told her if she ate the fruit she would be like God.**

Let's look at one more example of this progression. Let's take the story from the beginning of this chapter about Alexandra:

- Alexandra jumped off a bridge and took her life because…
- She didn't feel good enough; she felt like a failure, and she felt worthless. Because…
- She compared herself to others. Because…
- **Satan lied and told her she needed to be perfect and she fell for that lie.**

When we don't know who we are in Christ, we have no solid foundation. We have no compass to help us make wise decisions. And that is a really scary place to live from. When this happens, we tend to follow the crowd, make rash decisions, and make poor choices because we lack wisdom.

One of the foundational rules that I have chosen to live by is that I don't drive after drinking any amount of alcohol. None. Not even a sip. I do drink, in moderation, but I will not drink and drive. It is a decision I made many years ago.

In 2018, I was chosen to be on a jury for a trial involving a driver who hit and killed a pedestrian while drunk. This horrific case affirmed to me that I never want to operate a vehicle in an altered state. I live by this rule hard and fast, and all my close friends know I will not budge, even if the wine bar is just half a mile from my house. You see, I know what I stand for and why I stand for it, so I will not be tempted to make an unwise choice in these situations.

And to be honest, at thirty-seven years old, I still sometimes struggle with the desire to fit in, but when it comes to alcohol and driving, it doesn't even tempt me—I won't be shaken. How we live flows out of how we view ourselves. I view others and myself as precious children of God, and I don't ever want to risk hurting someone. Since that is one of my core beliefs and part of my identity, it keeps me from drinking and driving.

If we can help teenagers get a handle on their true identity in Christ, I sincerely believe they, too, will live out of that identity and make wise choices. This will give them the strength to stand firm in their convictions, no matter what the culture or their friends are saying or doing.

The other day, while driving to church, I pulled up behind a Tesla at a red light. I was admiring the car when I noticed something I'd never seen before on a Tesla: a bumper sticker! And believe me, I see a lot of Teslas in San Diego! I looked around and noticed that most of the vehicles near me had at least one bumper sticker on them. As I was taking all of this in, the Lord started to show me that this is an analogy of our worth and identity. The older cars around me had less value, and most of those cars had stickers on them—usually multiple stickers. But the "nicer" cars around me—the Teslas, Mercedes, Audi, BMWs, and Land Rovers—didn't have any stickers on them. As I thought through this, I also realized that I usually don't see kids and car seats in nice cars either. I was starting to connect the dots about what God was showing me.

With a luxury vehicle, because we know its value, we make wise decisions about where we drive the car, what we put on the car, who we let in the vehicle, where we park it, and so on. Humans are the same way. When we know our identity and our value in Christ, we take care of ourselves. We don't let just anyone into our lives, and we are careful about the people we spend time around. But when we don't know who we are or recognize our value, we allow things and people into our lives that can leave us hurt and devalued.

Our world is constantly telling us who to be, what to look like, and how beauty, brains, and bucks are the most important things in life. We are told to value these things above all else. And we are told that to succeed means to be the best in each of those areas. Every advertisement tries to sell us something that will help us succeed in one of those areas. This incessant bombardment is why we need to consistently help young people understand their true identity. Our students, just like us, can easily be distracted by someone or something and start to drift away from the truth of who they are.

That is why I always come back to the identity message. We need to remind young women of their worth to help them build a solid and firm foundation. When they choose to see themselves as God does and understand their great value, they will live life in a victorious way.

But remember that we as leaders also need to know, understand, and live out our value in Christ to model it for our students. Our identity is based in this: God—yes, the God of the Universe—sent His one and only Son to die for us. Each time I hear and read that, I am humbled and reminded of my identity and great worth.

How do we know what our identity is—and what it isn't? Ask yourself this question: "Can this change or be taken from me, or will it always be who I am no matter what I do or where I go?" If something can be taken from you or can change, don't find your identity in that. Here are some examples: soccer player, accountant, pastor, teacher, mother, wife, artist, and musician. Those things can change as we move through the seasons of life; therefore, none of those things are our true identity.

Every choice we make will be filtered through our identity—what we believe about ourselves. Believing—not just knowing, but deeply believing—our identity in Christ changes everything about us. I'm reminded of Meghan Markle, who was an actress in the United States with over two million people following her on social media. She was your typical actress who dressed like everyone else in Hollywood. All of that changed the minute she became British royalty by marrying Prince Harry. Once that happened, the way she dressed changed, her social media changed, her work changed, her friendships changed—everything changed because her choices were now filtered through her new royal identity.

We, too, have royal lineage, but ours is greater than Megan Markle's! Our Father is the King of the Universe, and we have royal blood flowing through our veins. That is our identity! If we can help our students believe this, I truly believe that their lives and their choices will change, too.

Don't ever forget who you are—and whose you are!

NOTE: At the end of the book, you'll find a list of thirty-three truths about who Christ says you and your students are—your true and never-changing identities!

Chapter 3 Summary

Plain and simple, when we don't know our
identity in Christ, we will struggle in life.
Knowing our true identity—who Christ says we
are—grounds us and gives us stability. When
we don't know who we are in Christ or we don't
believe it, we will make unwise choices because
we are unsure of our value—that was Eve's
struggle. Always remember who you are and
whose you are.

Chapter 4:

He's All About the Lies

Have you ever seen a photo of yourself and been shocked at what you were looking at? "That can't be what I really look like! That's not what I looked like when I left the house ... what happened?" Then, all of a sudden, the negative thoughts starting flooding your mind: you're ugly, you're fat, your arms are flabby, what's wrong with your hair, look at that double chin, your teeth are crooked, you are towering over everyone in the photo, that outfit is not flattering.

All of a sudden, your night is ruined because all you can think about is what you look like, which changes your mood and leaves you depressed. This has happened to me more times than I can count. As I look back, I get so upset that I allowed a photo of myself to dictate my night, my mood, and sometimes even my whole weekend.

It happens so quickly because the minute we agree with the first lie Satan feeds us, we open the door to him and his lies. Once I open the door to him, he rushes in and hijacks my thoughts. He knows if he can get me to focus on myself and the lies, I will isolate myself and shut down.

As an organization, we (Unveiling) always say, "How we live our life flows out of how we view ourselves, and how we view ourselves comes from our thoughts." I've heard it said that, on average, our mind thinks 70,000 thoughts a day, and out of those 70,000 thoughts, 80 percent (56,000) of those thoughts are negative. Yikes! What we think matters; it *really* matters!

One of the most important things our military does is study its enemies. Military leaders learn about strengths, weaknesses, potential moves the enemy will make, and how our enemies think. They need to know how to combat those who are out to hurt us in order to proactively protect us and keep us safe. Just like the military, we need to study our Enemy and learn how Satan works so we can effectively fight against his spiritual warfare.

Satan's battle strategy is to steal, kill, and destroy us (John 10:10). Scripture tells us in John 8:44-45 that lies are one of his greatest weapons and that there is no truth in him—he is the father of lies, and most of his lies come through our thoughts. Satan's job description is simple: He is a liar. I hate to admit this, but Satan is a good liar. He knows what lies we will fall for and the most opportune time to strike with those lies. He has been succeeding with this tactic since the Garden of Eden, and he is doing the same today.

Have you ever noticed how many verses use battle terms? It hit me the other day, and it was an "aha moment" for me. See the verses below that use battle terms and correlate with everything we are talking about in this book:

2 Corinthians 10:5 (NIV)

"We demolish arguments and every pretension that sets itself up against the knowledge of God, and we take **captive** every thought to make it obedient to Christ."

Ephesians 6:10-18 (NIV)

"Finally, be strong in the Lord and in his mighty power. Put on the full armor of God, so that you can take your stand against the devil's schemes. For our struggle is not against flesh and blood, but against the rulers, against the authorities, against the powers of this dark world and against the spiritual forces of evil in the heavenly realms. Therefore put on the full armor of God, so that when the day of evil comes, you may be able to stand your ground, and after you have done everything, to stand. Stand firm then, with the belt of truth buckled around your waist, with the breastplate of righteousness in place, and with your feet fitted with the readiness that comes from the gospel of peace. In addition to all this, take up the shield of faith, with which you can extinguish all the flaming arrows of the evil one. Take the helmet of salvation and the sword of the Spirit, which is the word of God. And pray in the Spirit on all occasions with all kinds of prayers and requests. With this in mind, be alert and always keep on praying for all the Lord's people."

Psalm 141:3 (NIV)
"Set a guard over my mouth, Lord; keep watch over the door of my lips."

Proverbs 12:18 (NIV)
"The words of the reckless pierce like swords, but the tongue of the wise brings healing."

2 Corinthians 10:3-6 (NIV)

"For though we live in the world, we do not wage war as the world does. The weapons we fight with are not the weapons of the world. On the contrary, they have divine power to demolish strongholds. We demolish arguments and every pretension that sets itself up against the knowledge of God, and we take captive every thought to make it obedient to Christ. And we will be ready to punish every act of disobedience, once your obedience is complete."

Romans 7:22-23 (CEV)

"With my whole heart I agree with the Law of God. But in every part of me I discover something fighting against my mind, and it makes me a prisoner of sin that controls everything I do."

The "aha moment" I had the other day was that I am in a serious war with Satan, and I can't take the battle lightly anymore. It might sound scary and overwhelming to hear this but let me reassure you that the battle belongs to the Lord (1 Samuel 17:47), and God wins in the end! We have the Creator of the Universe, the King of Kings, Lord of

Lord, our Father, our Friend, Redeemer, Savior, and our God on our side, and we do not need to fear!

I do want to be honest though: It will take hard work. It will even be exhausting at times. When we are creating new and healthy habits, it takes time, intentionality, determination, help from others, and lots of energy. Think about when you've tried to create a new habit. Maybe it was being on social media less, going to the gym more, eating healthier, watching less Netflix, or getting outside more. Trying to accomplish your goal took a lot of mental space, and it was hard work until it became second nature. Fighting off the lies takes the same work.

Also, remember, we were never meant to fight alone. You would never go to war alone, so don't fight these battles alone, and don't let your students fight their battles alone either!

Fighting our battles together reminds me of the story of Moses from Exodus 17. The Amalekites attacked the people of Israel while they were wandering in the desert. While Joshua led the troops into battle, Moses, along with Aaron and Hur, watched the action from a nearby hill. As long as Moses held up his hands, the Israelites would prevail, but whenever he lowered his hands, the Amalekites prevailed. Moses was getting exhausted battling the physical strain on his body by standing and keeping his arms in the air, and the story continues in verses 12-13 (CEV) and says, "Finally, Moses was so tired that Aaron and Hur got a rock for him to sit on. Then they stood beside him and supported his arms in the same position until sunset. That's how Joshua defeated the Amalekites."

That story is a beautiful picture of helping one another during battle. There will be seasons and times where we, and others, can fight off the lies by ourselves, and then there will be many times where we are exhausted and the battle is fierce, and we need an "Aaron" and "Hur" to help us out. May we be women who are courageous and share the lies we are struggling with and ask for help. And, may we be women who step in and become "Aarons" and "Hurs" for those who are struggling around us.

Like I mentioned above, Satan is the father of lies, and since that is his primary job, he is a good liar. Good liars are hard to catch because they are experts at manipulating and confusing their targets—the exact work Satan attempts in our lives. It's important to remember that Satan usually speaks in first person (using the word "I"), so it's harder to recognize his lies. If he were to say, "You are stupid," we would notice the lie and spot its source. But because he tends to speak in first person ("I am stupid"), it is harder to spot him—it feels like our voice instead of his. We must be on the lookout for our Enemy.

The older I've gotten, the more I've realized that Satan's lies aren't always logical. That's why it is so important to speak up and tells others what we're thinking and believing. As leaders, we need to create safe environments where students feel comfortable sharing with others and with us. Lies lose their power when they are exposed and brought into the light of God's grace, and a lot of times when we say what we are thinking, for the first time we "hear" the lie for ourselves and realize how crazy it sounds. If students are unable able to "hear" their lie, we as youth leaders have the opportunity to help them uncover it. Sometimes all it takes is someone who is not emotionally involved with the lie to see it for what it is and help the other person hear it correctly.

One lie that used to be all-consuming in my life (and had a very destructive effect on me) was the lie that I would only be beautiful if I were thin. I didn't just believe this lie; it had become one of my core beliefs. Core beliefs are what we think and believe about ourselves, other people, and the world we live in. They are things we hold to be absolute truths in the core of our belief system. They exist underneath all our surface thoughts. These core beliefs are so real and deep that everything in our life flows out of them.

Since my core belief was a lie, everything in my life flowed from that lie. In essence, I was living one big lie! Imagine how different my life would have been if my core belief had aligned with God's truth about beauty and body image!

The other day as I was reading Genesis 3:1-8, I realized that Satan only spoke to Eve twice. They didn't have a five-minute conversation. They didn't even have a one-minute conversation. Satan's conversation with Eve was about twenty seconds long—that's it. After the two lines Satan spoke to Eve, she took the words he had just spoken to her, she thought about them, accepted them, and then acted on them. Satan knows all he has to do is get us to stick around and listen to him, and once we do that, we will do the rest of the work for him. That's why it is vital to immediately shut the door, stop the conversation, rebuke him, and walk away. If we don't, we are very likely to be like Eve and receive, believe, and live out his dirty, ugly, and destructive lies.

When we believe Satan's lies, we don't simply believe them. We are accepting them and standing firm on them. It says in Matthew 12:30 (CEV), "If you are not on my side, you are against me." That means if we don't believe God's truth about who we are, then we are against God and support Satan and his lies. I know that can sound harsh, but once we believe and accept lies, we give Satan an open door in our life. That's why we must fight against his lies and do all we can to help our students reject his lies, too. Lies are never harmless; they are always destructive and hurtful. Our goal as youth workers is to help our youth form their core beliefs around Truth—God and His Word.

Over time, if you haven't rejected the lies and replaced them with the truth, you probably believe the lies as truth. That's why it can be hard to discern God's voice from the voice of Satan. The image below is a good tool to share with your students to help them figure out which voice they are listening to:

Satan's Voice	•—❤—•	God's Voice
Rushes		Stills
Pushes		Leads
Frightens		Comforts
Confuses		Enlightens
Discourages		Encourages
Worries		Calms
Obsesses		Peaceful
Condemns		Convicts

Have you ever noticed how natural it was when Satan suddenly appears to Adam and Eve in Genesis 3? Eve jumps right into conversing with Satan as if she was talking to Adam. This is one of the ways Satan works. He suddenly appears in our lives in a very natural way. That's why it is so important to know the difference between God's voice and

Satan's voice. Since he shows up unexpected, unwelcomed, and in a very sly manner, we need to be on guard and know what his voice sounds like.

The Bible talks about the power of the tongue in James 3:1-12, and I encourage you to pause for a moment, put this book down, and read that Scripture for yourself. Allow the Holy Spirit to show you new things and speak specifically to you through this passage before you keep reading.

Now that you are back from reading God's Word, sit for a minute and think about what James is saying. Our tongue, such a tiny part of our body, can cause great destruction. It is such a big deal that James gives us three different analogies to make sure we understand his message. He talks about a ship and the rudder, a horse and a bit, and a spark and a massive forest fire. Clearly, he doesn't want us to miss his point about understanding how powerful the tongue is.

After I read these verses, I was convicted and challenged to be even more careful about what I say to people. I was reminded that my words can do a lot of damage. We all need to be reminded of that. While James is talking in terms of what we say to others, I challenge you to think even more broadly about these verses. Yes, James is saying to be extremely careful about what we say, but he also says to be careful about what we think, read, and listen to because all of those things come in words.

James also talks about the power the tongue has over us, not just over others. James says the tongue can determine where our life goes—just by what we say and think about ourselves. A couple of years ago, I turned on a podcast to listen to while I was getting ready in the morning and someone said something in this podcast that stopped me in my tracks. It is a powerful statement, and it goes hand in hand with this passage. It states, "Whatever follows 'I am' will come looking for you." Here's an example of what that means. If you are constantly saying or thinking "I am not a good communicator," your body will follow those words you are proclaiming over yourself. Your body language will declare that you are not confident and comfortable when communicating. Your shoulders will most likely be slumped forward, you won't stand tall, and you will appear nervous and uncomfortable. You will probably also jumble your words and be a little shaky. Your body is doing what you told it to do. Clearly, whatever we are repeating and saying over ourselves can determine the direction of our lives.

I am too fat to wear these jeans.
No one likes me; I'm a loser.
I'm not pretty; I'm ugly.
I'm not coordinated; I'm a klutz.
I'm stupid.
I'm not good enough.

All of these statements have gone through my mind and come off my lips. When I listen to these kinds of lies and talk negatively about myself, it quickly becomes a bad habit. In those moments, I am choosing to focus on my feelings instead of the truth. Feelings are not always facts; sometimes they're just feelings. It takes hard work and dedication to change my ways. I have to fight to speak truth to myself.

We need to be extremely careful about the words we speak over ourselves because our words have power and give structure and direction to our life.

Our words can kill our hope … kill our self-esteem … kill our confidence … kill our desires … kill our joy … kill our peace … kill our beauty.

But take hope! They can also give us hope … give us self-esteem … give us confidence … give us desire …

give us joy … give us peace … give us beauty … give us freedom … give us life.

I finally came to the decision to believe who God says I am, no matter how I feel about myself. His words are our foundation, and we need to let God's words define us, not the lies that come through our negative thoughts.

I recently met with a young woman in jail. As I talked to her, God reminded me of the passage in James. This is the young woman's fourth time in jail, and drugs are her main struggle. As we were talking, she said, "I am a drug addict; that is who I am." I gently said to her, "I understand you struggle with drugs, but I want to encourage you not to say that anymore. What if you say you struggle with drugs and you are working on becoming sober? I don't want you locking yourself into that identity and giving power to it." She didn't quite understand the difference or why it even mattered, so I led her to James 3 and showed her what the Scriptures had to say about the power of our words. As I left that afternoon, I prayed and asked the Lord to encourage her and challenge her with what she thinks about and speaks over herself.

Satan wants to get us to a place where we hate ourselves, our lives, and God, and one way he does this is through his lies. When we believe his lies, we are thankless, unappreciative, and negative about who we are and how God created us. One practical way to ease people out of that mindset is to encourage those you are working with to be more grateful. I've firsthand seen the power of gratitude. When I practice it regularly, it improves my self-esteem. I believe the reason for this is I'm focusing on what I do have, not what I don't have. There have been many scientific studies done on gratefulness, and they have found that gratitude can change your brain! It's no wonder that 1 Thessalonians 5:18 (NIV) says, "Give thanks in *all* circumstances; for this is God's will for you in Christ Jesus." God knows that gratitude is a game-changer, and that's why He tells us it is His will for each one of our lives and to be grateful all the time.

I want to share a few of my favorite gratitude quotes with you because they are powerful:

"Gratitude interventions result in radical transformative improvements in personal wellbeing."
–Ann Voskamp

"The struggle ends when gratitude begins."
–Neale Donald Walsch

"Give thanks for a little, and you will find a lot."
–The Hausa of Nigera

"Gratitude turns what we have into enough."
–Melody Beattie

"Gratitude dissolves negativity."
–Sandi Krakowski

"Gratitude helps us to see what is there instead of what isn't."
–Annette Bridges

Encourage those you are working with to write down three things they are grateful for in their area of struggle every morning and every evening. Challenge them to find something new every day, and to look for the small things. Next time you meet, ask them to bring the list and share it with you. I bet it will not only start to reshape their brain but yours as well.

Our words have more power than we realize. Words have so much power that God created the world with His words, and He spoke life into existence with His words. We need to help our youth understand this and then help them make changes in their lives.

As we are helping the youth we work with, let's make sure they know we hear them and understand them, but let's also make sure we are not too shy to gently and kindly speak up and challenge them to be careful about what they speak and think over themselves. We don't want them speaking lies over themselves—we want them speaking truth, hope, and life!

Chapter 4 Summary

Satan's battle strategy is to steal, kill, and destroy us. Scripture tells us in John 8:44-45 that lies are one of his greatest weapons and that there is no truth in him—he is the father of lies. Satan's job description is simple: He is a liar. I hate to admit this, but Satan is a good liar. He knows what lies we will fall for, and he knows the most opportune time to strike with his lies. He has been succeeding with this tactic since the Garden of Eden, and he is doing the same today.

Core beliefs are what we think and believe about ourselves, other people, and our world. They are things we hold to be absolute truths in our belief system. They exist underneath all our surface-level thoughts. These core beliefs are so real and deep that everything in our life flows out of them.

Chapter 5:

Unveil

As I've already mentioned, I believe that almost everything we struggle with can be traced to a series of lies that we believe. I hope and pray this chapter will help you to come alongside students and help them figure out, and unveil, the root causes of their struggles.

Below are some good questions to ask young people about believing a lie. Reminder: Stay away from telling them what you think they are struggling with. Instead, help them discover the lie on their own if possible. But by all means, if they can't figure it out, please share with them what you discern as the true issue. When done in a sensitive way, this can help them get past their own blind spot.

- Who told you that?
- What will make you happier/more satisfied?
- What triggers this issue?
- What do you want that you are not getting?
- What are you getting out of this issue?
- Life is easy for people who obtain/look/have
  _____?
  - » What led you to think this? Where did those thoughts come from?
- And don't forget The 5 Whys from back in Chapter 2!

Here is an example of how you can use these questions in a conversation:

I am not pretty.

Who told you that?

No one.

So, where did that thought come from then? If no one verbally said it to you, did God say it to you?

No, God wouldn't say that! Hmmmm—maybe it was Satan?

I think you are on to something! What does the Bible tell us about Satan?

He is a liar—that is his job.

Does that sound like something he would say to discourage you?

Yes.

Then why do you not feel pretty? What has triggered this feeling in you?

I don't know. I look in the mirror and don't feel pretty. I don't look like the other girls.

So, it is a feeling you have—you don't FEEL pretty.

Yes.

Are feelings always facts or are they sometimes just feelings?

I think sometimes they are just feelings.

If you were to attain the "pretty" that you want to obtain, do you think that would make your life better, easier, and you'll be happier?

Yes.

So "pretty" girls have no problems and they always think they are pretty? They never struggle with their looks?

Well, no.

So, being pretty doesn't fix life's problems?

Well, I guess not.

Do you see the lie you're believing?

Yes.

What is it?

That pretty girls have no problems; life is easy for them. They have boyfriends.

That is not what I see of the "pretty" girls around me. It sounds like that is the same for you.

Yes.

Well, why don't you feel pretty enough? What has led you to this place?

I don't have a boyfriend.

So, having a boyfriend determines if we are pretty or not?

Maybe?

Do you have some pretty friends who don't have a boyfriend?

Yes.

Oh, so that isn't truth?

I guess not.

So, what is the truth?

Having a boyfriend doesn't determine if you are attractive or not.

I agree with you on that statement! What are you getting out of believing this lie?

What do you mean by that question? I don't think I understand.

We don't do something if we aren't getting something

out of it. This lie is feeding something in your life; you are getting something from it.

Oh, I think I understand what you are asking now. Hmmmm—well, when I believe that I am not pretty, I allow that to be the reason I do not have a boyfriend. If I didn't have that excuse, I would have to deal with the unknown of not knowing why no one wants to be my boyfriend. I'd rather have an excuse then not know why.

Yup, you totally got that question. You are getting a reason, and even though that reason/lie is discouraging and hurtful, you would rather sit in that than the truth that you don't know why you don't have a boyfriend.

After this, let her know that she will need to turn to God and His truth when she hears the lies. Remember, Hebrew 4:12 (CEV) says, "What God has said isn't only alive and active! It is sharper than any double-edged sword. His word can cut through our spirits and souls and through our joints and marrow, until it discovers the desires and thoughts of our hearts."

Several years ago, I had a hectic day, and I remember running from one meeting to another all day long. I had twenty extra minutes between two meetings, and I was close enough to my home that I was able to swing by my house to grab a snack and freshen up. As I walked into the bathroom to touch up my makeup, I remember looking in the mirror and groaning inside my head at what was looking back at me. It was not what I was hoping or wanted to see.

I touched up my makeup, turned around to leave the bathroom, and all of a sudden, the lies started bombarding me. Unfortunately, I had opened the door to them the moment I accepted the first lie I heard when I looked in the mirror, and now they were there to ruin my day. I very distinctly remember my shoulders slouching and the joy of my day being crushed instantly. Then, all of a sudden, I heard the sweet soft voice of the Holy Spirit, and He said, "Who told you that you are ugly?" I stopped in my tracks and said out loud, "Satan!" I knew it wasn't from God, so it had to be from Satan. That very moment I said to myself, "There is no way he is going to take over my day and win this battle. This means war!" I then started quoting Scripture out loud to combat the lies. I rebuked Satan and commanded him to leave. I asked God to forgive me for believing the lies, and in the car on my drive to the next meeting, I called a friend, brought to light what happened, and asked for prayer. After that phone call, my day turned back around, and I was set back on the right foundation.

After meeting with a girl who is struggling with lies, leave them with this, "When you hear something discouraging in your head, ask yourself, 'Who told me that?' Having to answer that question helps you to pinpoint where that lie came from. When we have to answer, 'Satan is saying that,' you can fight it because you don't want him to have power over you."

Someone may be struggling with a lie if you notice she has lost hope, or if she says anything about losing hope. We know we are under the influence of a lie when we lose hope. We have a living God who gives us living hope, so hopelessness is something that we can know is directly connected to Satan and his lies.

Also remember that most of our struggles are related to us comparing ourselves to others: weight, beauty, grades, friends, finances, popularity, fame, followers, likes, dating, God, parents, sex, and the list goes on. If students refuse to play the comparison game, many of their struggles can be eliminated.

One of the ways I fight the thoughts of not feeling enough is through contentment. Contentment is easy to talk about, but very rarely does anyone share how to live it out practically. How I get to the place of contentment in my life involves two things we have already talked about:

gratitude and focusing on what **IS** and not what isn't. When I can get my mind to stop looking around, focus on my lane, and seeing all that I do have, my heart quickly follows, and my spirits are lifted. I do this through writing it down, expressing it out loud to God, or calling a friend. It is imperative to hear yourself state your contentment because hearing it is very different than just thinking it. And, when you speak it out loud, Satan can listen as well, and that is one way to show him you won't fall for his lies. Contentment guards our hearts against not feeling enough, and that is a powerful truth we need to hold on to and teach others.

I've seen this in my own life through my travels to India. When I am home in the United States, I have to be on guard not to compare my weight or looks to anyone else. It is a constant battle here at home. But when I go to India, I don't struggle with this at all! Why is this? A couple of years ago I realized that I don't struggle with this in India because I look so ethnically different from the people there. It doesn't make sense to compare myself to them—it would be like comparing apples to bananas. You can't.

It is also because our culture values one body type and uses that body type in all advertisements. Since it does that, I am constantly feeling like I am not enough because I don't look like what is advertised. In India, they use all different body types, so I feel normal, like I fit in. But when I return to the United States and am around more people who look like me, it is like comparing a Red Delicious apple to a Granny Smith apple. It is easy to do, and everyone does it, whether they realize it or not.

The example conversation earlier in this chapter began with very strong feelings. But with a little help, the young woman quickly realized how destructive her thinking was. This is EXACTLY what we want to help girls understand. Satan's lies are crazy, and when we agree with his lies, we are accepting a crazy kind of thinking, too.

"Follow your heart" is a common phrase in our culture. I believe Satan is using that phrase to lead us astray and confused. I once had a big decision to make: Will I date this guy or not? I wasn't sure what to do, so I turned to my heart and followed its lead. I dated him. It felt so good. A few short weeks later, I realized what a poor decision I had made. I had followed my heart and my feelings and didn't rely on the Spirit's guidance.

Any time I hear the phrase "follow your heart" now, I want to scream, "NO, DON'T DO IT!" I have such a strong reaction because I've been let down by my heart way too many times. I don't trust or follow my heart anymore.

A song, movie, advertisement, or comment can shift my heart in less than a second. At a flip of a switch, my heart can go from loving and kind feelings to out-of-control and angry feelings. Feelings are not bad, but feelings are not always facts. Have you ever heard the phrase "Love is blind"? It means that when our heart is in love, we often are blind to reality and red flags. The feelings of love in our heart can overpower and fog up how we see life.

How many times have I done something that went against my morals and my core beliefs? How many times have I done something that I said I would never do? Unfortunately, I must admit that my answer is: "Often—I do those things often." Our hearts go against us because the root of our heart is sinful.

But don't be discouraged by this! God, who is perfect and all-knowing, promises to help us, guide us, and direct us, so we don't have to follow our heart. We have been given the gift of the Holy Spirit, and we get to follow the Holy Spirit as He guides us. And let me tell you, He is the best guide we could ever want! He knows us better than we do, He knows what is "around the corner," He looks out for our best interest, He is so for us, and He loves us! What more could you want in a guide?

So, instead of following our heart, let's be women who encourage the girls we lead to follow our wise, loving, kind, and caring Heavenly Father's heart!

We are here to help girls see life more clearly and see through Satan's attempts to confuse and trick them. That's what he did to Eve in the Garden of Eden, and he does the same with us. We all have blind spots, and we all need someone to gently help us become aware of our own so we can truly be free!

Chapter 5 Summary

Most of our struggles can be traced to a lie we believe. Help your students figure out the root cause of their struggle—in other words, help them unveil which lie(s) they are believing.

If they have lost hope, they are under the influence of a lie.

Chapter 6:

The "S" Word

Shame and lies go hand in hand. Shame is defined as a painful feeling of humiliation caused by foolish behavior, scandal, self-disgust, and embarrassment. Satan lies to us about who we are, and then he continues to lie and tell us that what we struggle with will always be who we are—that is when shame sets in. The worst part of shame is that it eats away at our soul. It convinces us that we are the worst version of ourselves. And it *destroys* our hope that we will ever find true peace.

Shame leaves us hopeless and defeated. Shame is the opposite of who God is and what He speaks over us. Romans 2:4 says that God's loving-kindness leads us to repentance. God showers us with love, kindness, grace, and hope—even in our ugliest moments of life! On the contrary, Satan lies to us, and his lies and shame lead us to feel hopeless, rejected, discouraged, and unloved.

Shame and guilt are often discussed in similar ways, but they are two distinctly different feelings. Shame says *I* am bad—it is my identity. Guilt says *what I did* is bad. Think of guilt in this way: If you were chosen to serve on a jury, you would sit through a court case and then deliberate with the other jurors to determine if the defendant is guilty or not. You decide by examining the law and the facts of the case, seeing if the defendant violated the law. Guilty simply means that a person violated the law.

Yes, we face consequences when we are guilty and violate man's law and God's law. We have to pay for what we do. But guilt should not make a young woman feel like she is a waste of a human being, a screw-up, and unworthy of man or God's love. If you ever see someone feeling that way, that is a great indicator that she is under the influence of lies and shame. (And don't be afraid or ashamed to deal with this if you see it in your own life!)

Examining the Bible reveals how God deals with shame. The minute Adam and Eve first sinned in Genesis, they felt shame, covered up, hid, and blamed each other.

God came walking in the garden looking for them, and He responded to them in love and kindness. God didn't shame them, yell at them, turn His back on them, or strike them. God asked them to confess what they had done and to come out of hiding.

That is exactly what God asks us to do when we start to feel shame. We have an incredible God who pursues us in our sin and shame, loves us in it, and wants to take us out of hiding from it. We must leave shame behind if we're going to walk in freedom and the truth of who God says we are. Shame will never lead us to God; shame will always pull us away from truth and God. You cannot be free and live in shame; that isn't true freedom.

I also love the story in John 8 when Jesus responded to a woman caught in the middle of having an affair. Jesus arrived on the scene, and the first thing He did was publicly respect the woman's dignity. He did this by dealing with the people who were shaming her. He told them that if they had not sinned, they could stone her. The accusers all dropped their stones and left. He forcefully, yet lovingly, put them in their place and let them know that He was the judge of this woman.

Then Jesus went over to her, met her at eye level, loved her, addressed her sin, and sent her on her way. I believe

Jesus had every right to let the people shame her and to shame her himself, but He didn't. That is not who He is, and He knows that shame doesn't work. He was not ashamed of her, and He has never been ashamed of us.

God steps into our sin and shame, and He does it without being annoyed or embarrassed by us. God walks toward us, loves us, and invites us out of it. God wants people to leave their life of sin and destruction and walk in newness of life, freedom, and abundance.

Shame tells us to shut up, be quiet, be ashamed, turn to an addiction to numb the pain, and hide the truth from others. That is so far from who God is—and so far from the people He created us to be. God is honored when we are honest with Him and others about our struggles. God honors us when we walk out of shame and darkness and into the light and truth. This is something that we must do, and this is something we need to encourage our youth to do as well.

Incarcerated women tend to have no shame. They put themselves out there, in every way, and they don't hold back. It is one of my favorite things about working with women behind bars. There are no masks or pretending to have it all together.

As I was leading a Bible study in jail a few months ago, we were reading the story of the adulterous women from John 8. At the end of class, I asked everyone what they got out of the lesson and how they can apply the Scripture to their own life. Some of the women shared how they need to stop judging people. Other women shared how grateful they were for a loving God who does not shame us and how they need to work on not shaming themselves. Then, all of a sudden, a woman who hadn't shared yet abruptly spoke up and said loudly, "I learned from this story that I need to stop sleeping with other people's husbands!" We looked at her with big eyes because that was not what we expected to come out of her mouth. After quickly processing what she just shared, I looked at her and said, "Thank you for sharing that. I appreciate your honesty and vulnerability. God is glorified in your response. God loves it when we are honest, and your transparency just brought Him honor!"

How beautiful is that! I can't imagine being at a Bible study with a bunch of people from church and someone being that honest. Yet, when we remove the shame, not only was she able to be honest, but all of us in the study accepted her, loved her, and appreciated her for her vulnerability. We didn't look down on her, but we looked up to her and now want to help her. To me, this is what the body of Christ should look like: a shame-free environment at all times.

So how do we help students remove the shame in their lives? We do it by helping them to do the opposite of Adam and Eve, who covered up, hid, and blamed each other. We need to teach girls to:

1. EXPOSE IT—bring it to the light and admit to God what they have done.
2. DESTROY IT—reject it and give the shame back to Satan.
3. OWN IT—confess it to someone. We were never meant to lead isolated lives or walk through hardships alone. Sins start to lose their power and grip on us when we bring them to the light.

God knows that if we are to move forward in healing, health, and the abundant life He has for us, He needs to champion us and believe in us. God will address our sin so we can deal with it and get it out of the way of our relationship with Him, but through that, He will shower us with His love and kindness. What an amazing Father we have!

Chapter 6 Summary

The worst part of shame is that it eats away at our soul. It convinces us that we are the worst version of ourselves. And it *destroys* our hope that we will ever find true peace. Shame leaves us hopeless and defeated. Shame is the opposite of who God is and what He speaks over us. Romans 2:4 says that God's loving-kindness leads us to repentance.

Chapter 7:

Life-Changing Truth

Do you really believe God's Word is 100 percent truth, 100 percent of the time? Do you really believe God's Word—the Truth—sets us free? Do you believe God's Word is alive and active and sharper than any double-edged sword? I am not saying you can never have doubts, but when helping young women fight lies, we have to be grounded in God's Word and believe the power the Word has!

It is important to recognize that the Bible is not a joyless set of rules and restrictions. God's Word is exciting and liberating! The Bible is the only book that is alive and active and is the pathway to truly knowing God on a personal level. We've seen its power firsthand; God's

Word has comforted us, healed us, convicted us, and set us free. Self-help books and positive affirmations are good and have a place, but those sources are not alive, active, or able to cut through our hearts like a warm knife cuts through butter. We need to continually remind ourselves how powerful the Bible is! What an amazing tool and asset God has gifted to us!

As a society, we love rescue stories. The theme of almost all great movies, books, and stories is rescuing. Think about it: *Titanic*, *Star Wars*, *Jurassic World*, *The Avengers*—these are all stories about epic rescues!

Although we have probably never needed a rescuing like *Titanic*, we have all needed rescuing in our lives. Maybe we locked our keys in the car, locked ourselves out of the house, got lost and needed directions, or ran out of gas. If you are anything like me, I need daily rescuing from the lies of Satan.

The word "rescue" is used over 400 times in the Bible. The Bible is one rescue story after another—that is why it is such a great read! Obviously, God is in the business of rescuing! And the greatest rescue mission ever told is when Jesus died on the cross. God sent His Son, Jesus, to die in *our* place and rescue all of humanity from hell.

God wants to rescue us from hell, but it is more than that. He wants to rescue us on a daily basis from life's dangerous and hard situations. Like I said before, God is in the business of rescuing and there is nothing He can't rescue you from. We are never, ever beyond rescuing!

If you were in a burning building, how many times would you cry out for help? Many times—continuously! You would cry out for help until you couldn't anymore. No one would stop because they were tired. There is no way you would shout for help once; you would keep calling for help until you were rescued. Likewise, we need to keep crying out for God's rescuing on a daily, hourly, and sometimes even minute-by-minute basis.

Take confidence in knowing that God cares about every lie you are facing in your life. You are never beyond rescuing. God will never give up on you. There is no lie that God does not want to rescue you from. But we must be careful to not only give Scripture as a response or answer to someone's questions or hurts. All of us have probably had someone quote us Scripture in an attempt to "fix" the problem we just shared with them, only to feel more frustrated and hurt by their attempt. There is a time for God's Word to be shared, but first, we need to be present and truly listen, acknowledge the other person's feelings, and demonstrate empathy. Share the truth of how God sees them, and *then* use Scripture to back it up.

We don't want to shove Scripture down someone's throat and make her feel bad for not believing it. We also never want to make other people feel ignored or overlooked. That is so far from how Jesus responded to those He encountered when He walked the earth. Jesus sat with people, listened to people, and wept with people.

When someone pushes Scripture on us, it can make us feel like we are not a good Christian. It can also make us feel unheard. That is not how God responds to us. God sits with us in our hurt, hears us out, comforts us, weeps with us, and then leads us back to Him.

Let's take a look at Luke 22:39-46. Would you please do me a favor and put the book down and read it for yourself before we continue?

I asked you to do that because God's Word is powerful and alive, and I wanted you to hear it directly from God. As you were reading, did you happen to notice that when Jesus went to the Father in deep agony, pain, fear, and worry before He went to the cross, God did not quote Scripture back at Him to help Him overcome the anxiety? God listened to Jesus, and then He gave Jesus an experience with Him.

Since we are to follow God's example of how to live, this is the perfect story for us to learn from. Jesus came to God with a very heavy heart, and He was emotionally hurting to the point that He sweat blood. God responded to Jesus by listening to Him and sending an angel to encounter Jesus and meet Him where He was at.

Let's take a minute to talk about when to share Scripture with others. First off, there is no formula. Life would be easier if God did that for us, but if that's how life was, we wouldn't turn to God and encounter Him. The answer to knowing when and what to share is to follow the Spirit's leading. You can't go wrong if you listen, obey, and do what He is telling you.

If you look at the story of Jesus battling Satan after He fasted for forty days (Matthew 4:1-11), we see that Jesus quoted Scripture several times when He was being tempted. The Scripture was deep in His heart, and when He needed it, it came to the forefront of His mind. He used it to get rid of Satan and his lies when He was alone.

We want to share Scripture with the young women we lead so when they are tempted and struggling, the truth will be in them and arise in their minds. We do not want to throw Scripture at them when they are in pain. Remember, as we just read in Luke, when Jesus went to

God with such a heavy burden, we see God respond by being present. Showing up, physically and emotionally, is one of the most important things we can do when someone is hurting.

I've noticed that we who follow Jesus (myself included) are really good at quoting Scripture, but we don't always know what the words actually mean. Here is an example of an often quoted and beautiful verse: *"I am fearfully and wonderfully made"* (Psalm 139:14 NIV). Several years ago, after being in ministry for quite a long time, I went to India with a group of young women to teach on the topic of identity. Our goal was to explain how to find true identity in Christ. With this verse as our text, I was easily able to explain what "wonderfully made" meant. But I was at a loss when I tried to define "fearfully made." To be honest, I had no idea what that phrase really meant. I sat down to pray through it and study it, and God revealed to me that night that it means God looks at us and is wowed by us (His creation) and our beauty.

We need to understand and be able to explain Scripture clearly or else we're doing a disservice to the girls in our ministries. It is okay if you don't have all the answers, but make sure you ask God, study, and ask others, so you are best equipped to help others.

Here is another popular phrase I hear and have used: "You need to find your identity in Christ." I remember hearing this in high school and even telling it to my friends and students over the years. Then one day I thought, "What does that even mean? It sounds Godly and cute, but what does it actually look like to do this? How can I explain it to young kids?" (If I can't explain it to little kids, I probably don't know what it really means.) So, once again, I sat down and prayed and studied and inquired of other believers. To my amazement, no one I asked could adequately explain to me what finding your identity in Christ truly means.

Finding your identity in Christ means you believe that what God says about you is truer than what anyone else, or yourself, says or thinks about you. Rick Warren, Pastor of Saddleback Church and author of *The Purpose Driven Life* says it means "That you abandon any image of yourself that is not from God ... You start believing what God says about you."

So, before we get ahead of ourselves, let's make sure we know the truth (we obviously won't know all of it) and let's make sure we can explain it simply.

Here's one of the most critical aspects of leaving behind the lies and living in the truth: We must learn to speak it OUT LOUD. I know it sometimes feels awkward to speak to ourselves out loud, but there is GREAT power in doing so. When we speak a truth out loud, we are not only saying it but also hearing it. We want to tap into as many learning styles as possible because that is how we all learn best.

Research has shown that talking to yourself out loud can motivate you to move forward with your goals, help you focus on a task at hand, and combat self-criticism. Gary Lupyan from the University of Wisconsin-Madison calls this phenomenon "feedback hypothesis." They recently did a study with athletes using the same strategy of having them speak out loud to themselves about their performance. The athletes would speak positive affirmations like "I will" and "I can" statements while they performed. These athletes ended up playing better than those who do not speak out loud. Imagine the difference if these athletes would have spoken God's Word over themselves! What an even more significant difference that would have made in their performance. As we've talked about, God's Word is alive and active and sharper than any double-edged sword, so speaking His words over ourselves will help us live better lives.

But it is more than that: It also is important to remember that Satan is NOT like God. He is not at all places at all times, he is not all-knowing, AND he cannot read our minds like God can. Since Satan cannot read our minds, when we quote Scripture to battle his lies in our head, he doesn't know because he can't hear them. That is why we must speak out loud. We don't need to yell at him, but we do need to use our voice (even if it's just a whisper) and let him know the truth we are proclaiming over ourselves. When we try to defeat the Enemy of our souls without using our voices, it is like trying to tell someone to stop doing something by only thinking about what we want them to stop doing. We need to speak God's truth over the girls, and we must let them know the importance of continually speaking it out loud over themselves, too!

Recently, I went to bed early because I was speaking at an event the next morning and I wanted to get a good night's rest so I'd have plenty of energy for the next day. As I got into bed, I grabbed my speaking notes and decided to go over them one last time. I was about five minutes into my notes when I got a text from a former student who I had run into in jail.

Five months earlier, I was in one of the local jails running a small group for the incarcerated women. The housing unit where we met is a transitional unit, so the women either are in and out pretty quickly or are transferred somewhere else rather quickly. That means I don't typically see the same women week after week. A deputy escorts the women to the room, and I meet with them for about ninety minutes.

Well, this particular week, the deputy brought the women in, and as I looked up to greet them, I recognized one of the faces. My heart started pounding, and I heard this young woman say, "I know you. I know you!" My heart sank and I smiled back at her. I knew her because she'd been in my ministry when I was a youth pastor. I didn't say much to her at the time because ten other girls showed up, and I didn't want to draw attention away from them and take time away from our class.

At the end of the class, when the deputy came back to escort the women back to their jail cells, this young woman walked up to me and started weeping. She said, "I know who you are; you were my youth pastor!" I told her, "I am not allowed to hug you, but I love you and I will be praying for you!" The deputy yelled, "Come on ladies, let's go!" and off she went.

My stomach was left in a knot, and I was unsure what to do. So, I prayed. I prayed, and I asked others to pray.

That night God reminded me that I used to pick her up and drop her off for youth group because her parents lived two streets over from me. I was ecstatic to be reminded of this! The next morning, I went to their house and asked if she was home (I didn't know if they knew she was in jail, so I decided to play dumb). They told me that she'd moved out years ago. They welcomed me in their home, to sit down and catch up. I went in and let them know she had been on my heart; they told me she was in jail and they had just found out. So, I told them the whole story about how I had encountered her in jail. They ended up giving me her new cell phone number and informed me that she was going to be released that very day. They were planning to pick her up and take her home.

That night I texted her and she responded immediately. She apologized for making such a mess of her life. She told me how hard jail had been and how difficult it was when she saw me there. She also confessed that after she was locked up, she discovered she was pregnant. Heavy stuff. I let her know I was there for her and want to stay in contact. She said she would love that and was thankful God allowed us to reconnect, even if it was in jail. She said it was a real wake-up call to see me there.

For five months, we texted periodically. She told me she wanted to meet up but never followed through. Still, she kept texting me. I just felt God saying, "Be persistent, but don't overdo it—stay connected." I would ask how the pregnancy was going, but she never replied to that question. I wondered if she had an abortion, and I didn't want her to feel shame if she did, so I finally stopped asking about the pregnancy.

This leads me back to the text I received from her when I was in bed prepping for my talk the next morning. It read, "I am five months pregnant and found out I am having twins. This morning I got an eviction notice, so my boyfriend and I decided to have an abortion. I just did … we just left. It was so traumatic, and I am so ashamed. I'm really depressed and feel extremely lost … more lost than I have ever been." I reread that text three times, thinking I must have misread it. "Is this real life—did I just receive this? I did—it wasn't a dream." Instantly, my heart hurt, and I ached for her. I couldn't imagine what she was going through; the whole situation was heartbreaking on so many levels.

So many emotions ran through me. I didn't know what to say or do. Then I heard the Lord say, "She just told you what she is feeling, so sit with her in it." And that is what I did. I let her know that I couldn't imagine the pain and trauma she was feeling. I let her know I heard her. I validated her. I just listened. Yet, I also was angry— angry at Satan for the lies he fed her that an abortion was the answer and that the lie led her to take the lives of two sweet, innocent children.

As I was awaiting her reply to one of my texts that night, I looked at my notes for the talk I was scheduled to give in twelve hours. All of my notes were on the topic of identity. The Lord said, "Now I want you to tell her who she is in me—her true identity." I have to be honest: I struggled with this. How could I tell someone who'd just walked out of an abortion clinic that God loves her, adores her, delights in her? Really—after killing two of His children? Suddenly the rubber hit the road. I had to ask myself, "Do I believe what I teach? Do I believe God's Word is 100 percent truth 100 percent of the time?"

I have reminded murderers in jail of their true identity and found it easy to do so. Why? Because I wasn't involved in the murder and the crime had usually occurred years prior. I did not talk to them as they were leaving the crime scene. I was completely removed from their situations.

But as I lay there, I looked at my notes again. I said to myself, "Yes, I do believe that God loves her, adores her, and delights in her. She is His precious child!" I then sent her a text letting her know all of this. After I sent it, the Lord reminded me of Romans 2:4, which tells us that God's loving kindness leads us to repentance. Shame doesn't lead us there, because shame doesn't work, but God's amazing love leads us back to Him. Not only did I know she needed to hear this, but I also needed to face the reality of how vast God's love is, how real and never-changing our identity is.

Do you believe this? Do you believe the truth about who you are and who others are, even in their worst state? This is why the truth—the Gospel—is so amazing. This is why it changes lives. At our worst, there is someone who unconditionally loves us, even when it makes no sense to us. That incredible love gives us the strength to pick ourselves up and continue to fight the good fight. There are no words for this crazy kind of love. And nowhere can we find such unconditional love other than from God.

Chapter 7 Summary

God's Word is 100 percent truth, 100 percent of the time. God's Word—the Truth—sets us free. God's Word is alive and active and sharper than any double-edged sword. When helping young women fight lies, we have to be grounded in God's Word and believe the power the Truth has!

Chapter 8:

The Journey Inward

I want to challenge you to pause and look inward at the core beliefs you accept about yourself—including any beliefs that are lies. I ask you to do this not only so you can be set free, but also because you'll be the most useful once you've done the work and experienced freedom yourself. And the reality is that we teach best through personal stories. Your students want to hear how you've overcome areas of struggle in your life. A personal story to back up what we teach is remarkably powerful!

Once I finally admitted to having an eating disorder, recovery required years of therapy. One of the things I loved the most about my therapist was that she had experienced the challenge of an eating disorder many years before I did. She went through recovery herself, so she was able to truly understand me. When I shared what I was thinking, feeling, and experiencing, she would ease my anxiety by telling me that what I was feeling was normal. She let me know that it was part of the healing process. Her stories and testimonies of overcoming and conquering her eating disorder were so powerful because they came from her personal life experience. It wasn't something she had learned in school or heard from another client—it was her personal journey that impacted me the most.

I encourage you once again to put this book down and ask the Holy Spirit to open the eyes of your heart and very clearly and specifically show you what lies you are believing. If you are having a hard time figuring it out, consider talking with someone close in your life who you will listen to and trust. Ask what they see and discuss your blind spots. Again, we all have them, and a lot of times they are hard to see.

Here are some good questions to ask yourself so you can discover what lies you may need to deal with:

What do you believe for others that you don't believe for yourself?

What do you tell others that you don't live by?

What do you publicly criticize in others that you secretly do yourself?

In what areas do you tend to get defensive?

Where do you feel like a failure?

What are you hiding?

Where are you overly controlling?

What can you not let go of or not do anymore—even healthy things?

If these questions made you aware of an area in your own life that needs addressing, ask God to lead you into His truth for you.

When I struggled with my eating disorder, I was obsessed with working out and had a deeply unhealthy relationship with the gym. I was also very controlling with what I ate, how much I ate, and where I ate. Food was always on my mind, and it always came up in conversation. I had no idea that I was struggling and had such an unhealthy relationship with the gym and food. Everyone on the outside could see I had a problem, but I was blinded by the lies I was living in.

Taking a close look at this mess—which had lasted for years—led me to discover my faulty core belief. I believed that if I was thin, then and only then would I be beautiful. Then I would be enough. Once I achieved the weight I wanted, I believed I would not have problems anymore.

What a false entanglement I was living in and how deep the issues were. I couldn't see them, but once I started asking myself the questions I listed, the blinders fell off, the veil was lifted, and the truth was revealed.

I now live with a core belief that is rooted in God's truth, which gives me the freedom to be healthy with food and exercise. I no longer feel the need to judge myself or others.

I encourage you to press in, put in the time, and do the work to overcome the lies and core beliefs you live with. You are not meant to overcome the lies alone, so make sure you reach out to a pastor, counselor, or mentor who can walk this journey with you. It is okay to be in ministry or be working with youth and also be going to counseling or dealing with hard stuff—our weaknesses and hardships don't disqualify us from working with youth. Satan will lie to you and tell you to stay quiet but fight against that and press into the difficult so you can become healthy.

I don't know about you, but running is hard for me—like, really hard. I'm pretty sure when people see me running, they think, "That girl looks like she is in pain!" When I run, I am fighting the whole time to keep my body moving. Nothing about running comes naturally for me—nothing!

There is a Scripture that talks about running a race, and it talks about struggling while running. I love how the Bible accurately and honestly describes this race that we call life as difficult—we have to fight to move forward and stay the course. It is not going to be natural for us to do the right thing. We are going to be swayed and distracted by other people "running" in their lanes next to us, and it will be tempting to join them.

Here's the deal: God calls us to look up and run the race He has set out for us. Just like in physical running, we don't run and look to our left and right; as we run, we look at our goal ahead of us.

While running, if you look at the lanes to the left and right of you, one of two things will happen: Either you will eventually end up in the other person's lane, or you will trip and fall. The reason you would end up in the lane next to you is because wherever we fix our eyes, our body and life follow. You would trip and fall because your eyes are not focused on what is ahead of you, and you would not see the obstacles coming at you.

That is just like real life. As it says in Hebrews 12:1, "Let us throw off everything that hinders and the sin that so easily entangles [us]" (NIV). There are times when we are running our race, looking toward Jesus and living for Him, and we get distracted by the temptations, addictions, unhealthy relationships, or other diversions in the lanes next to us. And if we are not proactive and careful, the sin and distractions will entangle us. That's why we MUST keep looking up at Jesus, so we don't end up tripping, falling, and entangling ourselves.

There are other times when we are steadily running our race and people and/or things wander into our lane, without invitation. We have to take those things and quickly push them out of our lanes so we don't lose our focus and goal of looking up at Jesus.

Let's run this race together, fighting, struggling, and straining toward the goal: the abundant life that God has waiting for us! Fight on, sister!

Let's also work on discipline. I know the word "discipline" isn't sexy, but it is a good word that keeps us on track, healthy, and balanced. Dictionary.com defines discipline as "Activity, exercise, or a regimen that develops or improves a skill; training." I'm taking a wild guess here, but I think all of us want our minds and hearts full of life-giving truth, not destructive lies. We will not mysteriously wake up one day and be full of truth, accept the truth, and only think God's truth over ourselves. The only way we will get to a place of naturally grabbing hold of the truth and throwing away the lies is through discipline: control, education, work, development, practice, self-control, and preparation.

Working on ourselves is a lifelong journey. I thought after I got out of recovery that I was done. I had put in thousands of dollars, endless time, and all my energy, so I should be good to go now! Nope. Other things started popping up in my life that I wasn't aware of. I believe life is meant to be this way because when we see our weaknesses and challenges, we are more apt to turn to God and recognize our need for Him, and that is exactly what He wants from us: to continually be turning to Him and relying on Him.

Also, when we don't deal with our "stuff," we start to push our pain and problems on others. Maybe you have heard the phrase "Hurt people hurt people." When we have unresolved issues, they seep out of us and get forced on those around us. We need to make sure we are dealing with our stuff so we don't accidentally push our problems on our students. I can't tell you how many times I have seen that happen. It usually comes from parents who didn't deal with their pain and then unknowingly transfer that to the child. Let's make sure we aren't doing that to the youth God has placed in front of us.

As real as the phrase "Hurt people hurt people" is, the phrase "Healed people heal people" is just as true! Run toward healing so you can help those around you deal with the hurt in their lives. It is hard work, but it is worth it. I truly believe God can use us more effectively to further His Kingdom when we are healthy. Let's fight the good fight together. Let's be the best we can be for the youth God has entrusted to us!

Chapter 8 Summary

You'll be the most useful once you've done the work and been set free yourself. Press in, put in the time, and do the work to overcome the lies and core beliefs that you live with. You are not meant to overcome the lies alone, so make sure you reach out to a pastor, counselor, or mentor who can take the time to walk this journey with you. It is okay to be in ministry or be working with youth and also be going to counseling or dealing with hard stuff—our weaknesses and hardships don't automatically disqualify us from working with youth.

Chapter 9:

Deep in the Heart

I came across this quote years ago, and it remains one of my favorites,[3] "If you want to learn something, read about it. If you want to understand something, write about it. If you want to master something, teach it." I wholeheartedly believe this, and this is the goal of our ministry. We all know that this quote is true because we have experienced it in school. Most of us learn very little when we are strictly lectured to, but as we add more and more of the different teaching styles to our learning, we

---

3   Yogi Bhajan

take it in, and it sticks. This also applies when we work with students.

In our ministry, we have conferences and events for girls to attend every year. At *every* event or conference, each girl leaves with a devotional and/or tool that can be used to follow up on what they learned at the event. Not only do we do this for young women, we also do this with the incarcerated women, and the women in India we work with as well.

In addition to the events and conferences we hold, and the follow-up material we give teenagers to remember and apply what they learned, we offer one-day Mexico missions trips several times a year. We are fortunate to live only forty-five minutes from the Mexican border, so it is easy for us to do this. On each trip, the girls visit an orphanage, where they have the opportunity to teach what was taught to them at our conferences and events. We also take a trip twice a year to India and they do the same thing there. The India trip is two weeks long, and instead of teaching in an orphanage, we teach in schools. It's such a joy to see our students teach girls their own age about their worth and identity in Christ!

I love these trips because I get to see the girls truly internalize things they have learned through our teaching.

They take the time to learn for themselves and figure out how to explain it to someone who speaks English as a second language. I can see them share this knowledge straight from their own hearts.

This is where I want to challenge you to take it to the next level. Where can your students go to share their stories and teach others about their struggles and the truths they've learned? Where can they go to help someone else? We need to remind them that they do not have to conquer their own issues 100 percent before God uses them to help others. We are all in the process, and sometimes people just need to hear from someone who is a few steps ahead of them; it is more relatable and powerful for both parties involved.

You might suggest to your students that they consider mentoring someone who's younger than them. You could offer to go with them to guide them—*but make sure you let them lead*. Encourage them to teach in the children's ministry at church so they can share with kids and learn how to talk about God's truth in simple terms. Have them practice sharing by first writing their story down or sharing it verbally at their Christian club at school. Encourage them to share during a testimonial time in the youth group. Video them and encourage them to post it on social media with some follow-up questions for people to think through. There are endless ideas. Be creative. Be intentional.

Remember that story is powerful! That's why the students need to get out there and share theirs. Stories are compelling and captivating—they help us relate to one another, keep us engaged, and they are easy to remember because our emotions get involved with the learning. Much of what Jesus taught was done through stories because it worked. Messy stories are okay—we all relate to messy. Students sharing their stories will also help them to realize that God is using them—and that God's purpose and plan are at work in their lives.

Sharing with others provides great incentive for us to live out what we teach. We all want to be people who walk the walk and talk the talk.

Yet, there is also a surprisingly risky side to telling our stories. When we teach and share God's truth, Satan may attack us in the very area of life where we are experiencing victory. In fact, we can expect him to. That is exactly what spiritual warfare is: our enemy trying to take back the ground he has lost to God's truth. Our students need to know that if they slip up or struggle, they do not have to face it alone. You and others are there to offer support.

Spiritual growth involves breaking the cycle of secrecy that keeps us in bondage. Regularly and intentionally ask your students how they are doing in the areas where they struggle. Remind them that it is okay if they mess up. It is okay to be an imperfect person who still sins. There is no shame if that happens—we are all human. Satan will want to keep them in the darkness of shame, and he will consistently whisper to them to fight it alone. We all know what happens when we do that: The issue gets worse and worse, and we end up in a dark place. And when people keep their areas of struggle and shame hidden, that's when lives and ministries get ruined.

I have seen this happen firsthand. Someone didn't speak up because she thought she could fight it alone. She was too embarrassed and ashamed, so she stayed quiet. And when it finally came out, like it always does, it ruined her life and affected countless other people's lives as well.

God is honored when we humble ourselves and confess what is going on in our lives.

Chapter 9 Summary

"If you want to learn something, read about it. If you want to understand something, write about it. If you want to master something, teach it."[4]

Chapter 10:

Fight for Freedom

"Freedom: unrestricted, released from something difficult, without hindrance, liberation from the power of another." Reading this definition of freedom makes me want to fight with all I've got to obtain freedom in my own mind, heart, and life. It makes me want to yell "FREEDOM!" at the top of my lungs like Mel Gibson in the movie *Braveheart*. Nothing feels as good in life as being truly free!

If you have ever been in bondage or bound to something—a home, diet, addiction, unhealthy person, debt—then you know how all-consuming it can be. You literally feel chained to it, and it feels like it follows you wherever you go. It restricts you from being free in mind and body, and it keeps you from living the full and abundant life God has for you.

Galatians 5:1 says, "Let me be clear, the Anointed One has set us free—not partially, but completely and wonderfully free! We must always cherish this truth and stubbornly refuse to go back into the bondage of our past" (TPT). I love how this verse reminds us that freedom is not partial. Real freedom is when we are completely, 100 percent free! I also love the verse's reminder that we must fight and refuse to go back to the bondage of our past. That means we are going to have to fight to keep our freedom. It is not an easy road because we get pulled into Satan's lies so easily. And the Enemy is always there ready to tramp us, tempt us, and trick us by convincing us that our old ways of bondage are a better option than the path to freedom. Always remember that Satan's job is to lie to us—and he never tires of the battle. We must always keep fighting for our freedom.

This can be exhausting and daunting at times. But fighting for our freedom is much like working out. The more we work out, the more strength we build, and the easier it gets. The more we fight Satan, the more knowledge and strength we build, and the easier that gets as well.

The more we fight, the more operating in truth becomes our new way of thinking and acting—our new natural response. What was once exhausting no longer is—and victory becomes our new normal.

Bondage keeps us from doing what God has called us to do and being who God has called us to be. When something in life keeps us in bondage, we cannot fully do what God has called us to do. Scripture reminds us in Matthew 6:24, "How could you worship two gods at the same time? You will have to hate one and love the other, or be devoted to one and despise the other. You can't worship the true God while enslaved to the god of money!" (TPT). We cannot love two things at the same time. We cannot believe and live in the truth of who God says we are while simultaneously believing and living in the lies that Satan feeds us. One will always have priority. Jesus reminds us that we cannot be a slave and be free at the same time. Without freedom, we are held back in life, and I don't know anyone who wants to be held back.

Sometimes it's hard for me to see those things that enslave me. But why? Why is it so tough to know what is keeping me from being free? Sometimes it is difficult to know if we are enslaved because those things have become our normal. A lot of times other people can see what's happening, but we find it comfortable. We have cozied in it, welcomed it, and learned to accept it. To be frank, we kind of like it (though, if we're honest, we probably have a love/hate relationship with these struggles).

Believe it or not, freedom can be scary. I've seen this with the girls in jail. When they are about to be released, they can't sleep at night because they're so excited. But they're also scared. Because it has been so long since they experienced freedom, it becomes an unknown world to them. And the unknown is always a bit frightening.

This can also be true when we help walk people into freedom. It is an unknown, and most of us don't like unknowns and new things. When people have operated in bondage and lies for so long, the newness of freedom becomes scary.

We need to ease people into freedom for this exact reason. Living in freedom may be a new method of operating, and change takes time. The young women we work with need to learn new habits and how to operate in their newfound truth—it doesn't happen overnight. But experience has shown me that once these women have tasted freedom, they won't need any more convincing to let go of their old ways and cling to their newfound freedom.

The battle for freedom was never meant to be fought alone. So, jump in the ring, put up your dukes, and fight for yourself and your students with all you've got! Our sisters need a coach, a cheerleader, and a partner to fight with them—and you are called for such a time as this!

Chapter 10 Summary

Galatians 5:1 says, "Let me be clear, the Anointed One has set us free—not partially, but completely and wonderfully free! We must always cherish this truth and stubbornly refuse to go back into the bondage of our past" (TPT). Freedom is not partial. Real freedom is when we are completely, 100 percent free!

Closing

Recently, a former student called me asking for help. She's now a youth leader and needed guidance for how to deal with her students and their struggles. She asked me, "Do you know of any books I can go through with these girls? They are all dealing with different issues, and to be honest, I don't know what to say or do. I need help!" I listened to her frustrations and feelings of inadequacies and told her that, unfortunately, I didn't know of a book, but I could give her some tools to help her out. I proceeded to share the tools that are listed in this book, I encouraged her, and I told her to look back on her life and think through what helped her get through hard times. By the end of the conversation, she realized she had the tools she needed, and she felt confident and equipped to help these girls.

Two weeks went by and I contacted her to check in and see how she was doing. She said, "Things are going really well, actually. Our conversation really helped me stop complicating things and focus on being consistent with them."

I love what she said: stop complicating things. Sometimes we feel like we have to "fix" another person or find the "right" book to take her through, but a lot of times we simply need to show up, be a good listener, ask good questions, and be consistent. As I look back on the youth leaders and mentors in my life, none of them fixed me, but all of them spent time with me, listened to me, challenged me, and followed up with me.

You are capable. If God has called you to work with youth, then you have what it takes, and the Holy Spirit will continue to teach you and give you what you need when you need it! Don't believe the lies that tell you otherwise!

Your True Identity

It doesn't matter what you believe or what you do;
this is who God says you are:

ACCEPTED

God knows everything about you—all your thoughts,
words, deeds, and attitudes—and He still accepts you and
loves you!

*"Honor God by accepting each other, as Christ has accepted
you" (Romans 15:7 CEV).*

BEAUTIFUL

Beautiful is defined as "pleasing to the senses." That means
that not only are you physically beautiful, but your smile
is beautiful, your voice is beautiful, your personality is
beautiful, and your kindness is beautiful. Every aspect of

you was intentionally and uniquely designed, and all of you is stunningly beautiful!

> *"You are altogether beautiful, my darling, beautiful in every way" (Song of Solomon 4:7 NLT).*

BELOVED

You're not just loved by God; you are *dearly* loved by God! You are darling to Him, and He holds you close to His heart. You are God's beloved!

> *"Look with wonder at the depth of the Father's marvelous love that he has lavished on us! He has called us and made us his very own beloved children" (1 John 3:1 TPT).*

CHERISHED

God values you. He deeply cares about you and what you care about. He holds you close to protect you, and He can't keep His mind off of you. God cherishes you!

> *"The LORD will take delight in you, and in his love he will give you new life. He will sing and be joyful over you" (Zephaniah 3:17 GNT).*

CHOSEN

You are chosen: highly favored, preferred, special. And you are not only chosen by God, but God intentionally handpicked you!

"Do not fear, for I have redeemed you; I have called you by name; you are Mine!" (Isaiah 43:1 NASB).

COMPLETE

God only creates the best, and He leaves nothing unfinished. You are a complete creation. You don't need to be taller, thinner, prettier, smarter, or more popular. You lack nothing.

*"And in Him you have been made complete"
(Colossians 2:10 NASB).*

ENOUGH

Comparison says you don't measure up—you're not smart enough, thin enough, pretty enough, popular enough, or good enough. God says you don't fall short in His eyes. You—as you are—are enough!

"You made all the delicate, inner parts of my body and knit me together in my mother's womb. Thank you for making me so wonderfully complex! Your workmanship is marvelous" (Psalm 139:13-14 NLT).

FREE

Through Jesus' death on the cross, you are free. Free from sin and death. Free from the opinions of others. And free to be unapologetically you. Don't let your insecurities, worries, and mistakes hold you back from enjoying all that God has for you. Freedom is freely yours!

"The Anointed One has set us free—not partially, but completely and wonderfully free! We must always cherish this truth and stubbornly refuse to go back into the bondage of our past" (Galatians 5:1 TPT).

GIFT

You are a gift, and you are needed in this world: your smile, your humor, your one-of-a-kind personality. And not only are you a gift, but God has given you unique gifts to share with others.

"Your very hands have held me and made me who I am"
(Psalm 119:73 TPT).

HEARD

God hears you and never turns away from you. He absolutely loves listening to you, and you have His full attention—all the time!

"Then when you call, the Lord will answer. 'Yes, I am here,'
he will quickly reply" (Isaiah 58:9 NLT).

KNOWN

God knows about every area of your life—the good, the bad, and the ugly. And not only are you known for who you truly are, but God also knows you better than you know yourself. He completely understands you and loves you.

"You have looked deep into my heart, LORD, and you know
all about me. You know when I am resting or when I am
working, and from heaven you discover my thoughts. You no-
tice everything I do and everywhere I go. Before I even speak
a word, you know what I will say" (Psalm 139:1-4 CEV).

MASTERPIECE

You are a work of outstanding artistry. God dreamed you up, and then He took His time to design you carefully. God only creates beautiful things, and YOU are an extraordinary masterpiece!

"And yet, O LORD, you are our Father. We are the clay, and you are the potter. We all are formed by your hand"
(Isaiah 64:8 NLT).

PURSUED

God relentlessly pursues you on a daily basis. No matter where you go or what you do, God will always chase after you. There is nothing you can do to stop Him because you are that important to the Creator of the world.

"Surely your goodness and unfailing love will pursue me all the days of my life" (Psalm 23:6 NLT).

ROYALTY

Because of God, you have royal lineage and royal blood flowing through your veins; your status is *Princess*! You are a daughter of the King—and not just any King, but THE KING!

"And since we are his true children, we qualify to share all his treasures, for indeed, we are heirs of God himself" (*Romans 8:17 TPT*).

SEEN

God sees all of you: your hurts, worries, struggles, desires, and dreams. God sees all of you, and He genuinely cares about all of you. Nothing about you and your life is overlooked. You are seen! You are known! You are loved!

"'You are the God who sees me,' for she said, 'I have now seen the One who sees me'" (*Genesis 16:13 NIV*).

CITIZEN OF HEAVEN

You legally belong to Heaven if you have accepted Christ as my Savior. You currently live in a foreign country but eagerly look forward to your eternal home, where there will be no more tears and where you will be with my King and Father forever. Earth is not your home; the Kingdom of Heaven is where you belong. You are a citizen of Heaven!

"But we are citizens of heaven, where the Lord Jesus Christ lives" (*Philippians 3:20 NLT*).

WANTED

God wanted you before your parents ever considered having a child. God yearns to spend time with you. God wants to include you in all He is doing. God doesn't do it out of obligation; He does it because He genuinely likes you. The lover of your soul desired your existence so much that He uniquely handcrafted you so He could spend time with you. You are deeply wanted!

"God called me by his grace; and in love, he chose me from my birth to be his" (Galatians 1:15 TPT).

WELCOMED

God excitedly welcomes you into His presence. There is nothing you could do and say, and nowhere you could go that would stop Him from welcoming you to be with Him. He never shuts the door or turns His back on you. He has—and will always have—the door open for you to come in. You are always welcomed in by God!

"But everyone my Father has given to me, they will come. And all who come to me, I will embrace and will never turn them away" (John 6:37 TPT).

GOD'S CHILD

You are God's child; you are His daughter! He is a good Father and the perfect Father. He is your pillar of strength and support. God is gentle; He is kind. He is never ashamed of you. He loves you and calls you His own. You are God's precious child.

"All of you are God's children because of your faith in Christ Jesus" (Galatians 3:26 CEV).

FRIEND OF GOD

God not only calls you His creation, but He also calls you His friend! He not only loves you, but He likes you, too! You are the King's friend. You are God's friend. You are the Creator's friend. You are a friend of God!

"I have never called you 'servants,' because a master doesn't confide in his servants, and servants don't always understand what the master is doing. But I call you my most intimate friends, for I reveal to you everything that I've heard from my Father" (John 15:15 TPT).

NEW CREATION

God doesn't remind you of your past faults; instead, He reminds you of how He is transforming you into a new creation. God wants to help you get rid of the old you—the broken and messy parts—and help you become the better you, the best you!

"Therefore, if anyone is in Christ, the new creation has come: The old has gone, the new is here!" (2 Corinthians 5:17 NIV).

PRICELESS

Your life and body are so precious that their value cannot be determined. Jesus, who was innocent, died for you. You were guilty, but He took your place. There are no price tags on you because you are priceless!

"You were God's expensive purchase, paid for with tears of blood, so by all means, then, use your body to bring glory to God!" (1 Corinthians 6:20 TPT).

FORGIVEN

Because of Jesus' death on the cross, if you ask God to forgive you, He will do it without hesitation, because there is no sin that God won't forgive. You can forget what is behind and move forward in Christ's forgiveness and freedom. You are fully forgiven!

"Put up with each other, and forgive anyone who does you wrong, just as Christ has forgiven you" (Colossians 3:13 CEV).

TEMPLE OF THE HOLY SPIRIT

The Holy Spirit doesn't live in fancy gold temples, expensive buildings, or large shrines. Instead, He lives in you because you are worth more than anything a person can make. The Holy Spirit chooses to dwell in you because you are *that* special!

"All of you surely know that you are God's temple and that his Spirit lives in you" (1 Corinthians 3:16 CEV).

CREATED WITH A PURPOSE

As God was knitting you together, He created a highly specific plan for your life that no one else has. His plans are unique to you and were made just for you. He sets you apart from the ways of the world and calls you to bigger, greater, and more exciting plans than you could ever dream of. You have a special calling on your life that only you can live out!

"'For I know the plans I have for you,' says the LORD. 'They are plans for good and not for disaster, to give you a future and a hope'" (Jeremiah 29:11 NLT).

NEVER ALONE

You are never ever alone. God is always with you. God enjoys you so much that He doesn't want to be away from you. Through thick and thin, you always have a companion with you!

"This is my command—be strong and courageous! Do not be afraid or discouraged. For the LORD your God is with you wherever you go" (Joshua 1:9 NLT).

REDEEMED

God takes all your mistakes and faults that have caused you harm and He restores them. He loves to take what seems ruined and wasted and turn it into beauty and purpose. He won't give up on you, and nothing in your life is lost. Nothing is worthless. Nothing is wasted. Your life is redeemable!

"Since we are now joined to Christ, we have been given the treasures of redemption by his blood—the total cancellation

of our sins—all because of the cascading riches of his grace"
(Ephesians 1:7 TPT).

MORE THAN A CONQUEROR

Through Christ you can conquer anything because the One who has conquered death lives in you. You don't just achieve victory, but you are overwhelmingly victorious with Christ's help!

"In everything we have won more than a victory because of Christ who loves us" (Romans 8:37 CEV).

BEAR GOD'S IMAGE

God can't physically be seen, but He created you to look like Him; you are a visual representation of God. When God uniquely handcrafted you, He wove part of Himself into you. You are like a mirror that reflects God so others can see Him through you in love and creativity, through the way you live intentionally, morally, and socially. You are the visual image of God!

"So God created human beings in his own image. In the image of God he created them; male and female he created them" (Genesis 1:27 NLT).

UNCONDITIONALLY LOVED

You are deeply loved no matter what you do, where you go, what you say, or what you believe. God loves you passionately, and nothing will separate you from His love. There are no conditions to His love; He offers just immense lavish love—all the time!

"God saved you by his grace when you believed. And you can't take credit for this; it is a gift from God"
(Ephesians 2:8 NLT).

AMBASSADOR OF CHRIST

God intentionally handpicked you to be His spokesperson to the whole world! He knew you were the right person for the job, so He chooses you daily to represent Him and His love. You are God's promoter; you are an ambassador of Christ!

"God has given us the task of telling everyone what he is doing. We're Christ's representatives"
(2 Corinthians 5:20 THE MESSAGE).

CAPABLE

Through Christ, you have the qualities—physical, mentally, spiritually—to accomplish what God has set out for you. You can do what God puts in front of you—and do it well! The same power that raised Jesus from the dead lives inside of you, and He wants to help you accomplish what seems impossible. You are able!

"I find that the strength of Christ's explosive power infuses me to conquer every difficulty" (Philippians 4:13 TPT).

PROUD

God is *never* embarrassed by you. He is not ashamed of who you are. He is proud to call you His own—no matter what you have or have not done. God boldly proclaims to the world that you are His!

"Look with wonder at the depth of the Father's marvelous love that he has lavished on us! He has called us and made us his very own beloved children" (1 John 3:1 TPT).

About the Author

R ondi has worked in full-time youth ministry since 2003. In 2008, she created Unveiling (unveilinglies.org) and it was birthed out of her own pain and battles. She initially developed Unveiling as a conference for high school girls in Southern California and now it has grown into an organization that works with young women all over the  world, as well as incarcerated women.

Rondi has a huge heart for young women because she remembers how difficult those years can be. She believes that during junior high, high school, and college, the decisions girls make can greatly influence who they become. Rondi has been sought after by many churches, schools, and nonprofit organizations to guide them in knowing what young women are going through and how to help them handle these issues. She has a pulse on the struggles young women face and is passionate about equipping them to win their battles.

Rondi loves the sunshine and being active, so San Diego has been the perfect home for her! She enjoys adventures and traveling, especially internationally, and her favorite home away from home is India. Out of all of her names, her favorite is, "Auntie Rondi" and "Liberty Love"!

About Unveiling

Women of all ages are confronted with destructive lies about their identity and worth every day. It is the mission of Unveiling to expose lies, reveal truth, and help women fight lies through live events, written materials, and social media. As a result, they are set free from the bondage of the lies so they can flourish in their true identity.

AMERICA

Hundreds of eighth- through twelfth-grade girls gather for our yearly events. It is here that we remind them of their true identity and worth. This is important to us because everything we do in life flows out of how we view ourselves, and most girls have a distorted view of themselves. We also write materials for the girls to take home so they can continue to be reminded of the message of truth after they leave our events. We have a presence on Instagram as well so we can daily encourage them in their identity and worth.

MEXICO

Unveiling travels down to Mexico about six times a year. We train young women from America to share the same truths that we teach at our U.S. events to Mexican girls at orphanages. We also host a one-day event every year for teen girls in Mexico. These events have the same purpose as our American events.

INDIA

Unveiling also has a presence in India. We travel to India twice a year. In local schools in India, using cultural sensitivity and understanding, our American girls share what they have learned through Unveiling with Indian girls who are their same age. We are also in the process of creating a year-long Unveiling program in India that will be run by the locals in their communities.

JAIL

We lead several small groups every month with incarcerated women in San Diego County. Each participant of the small group is given an Unveiling devotional, so they can continue to grow in their identity in Christ. We also host four worship concerts a year for the women. We are very intentional at these concerts to include songs that speak messages of truth.

As a lead-in to each song, we remind the women of their great worth, and we offer encouraging words.

Find out more about Unveiling by visiting:
unveilinglies.org & @unveilinglies

You can find gratitude journals, identity cards, devotionals, and more in the online store.

Resources

NATIONAL SUICIDE PREVENTION LIFELINE:
1-800-273-8255
You don't have to be in crisis to call or text! The Lifeline provides 24/7, free, and confidential support for people in distress, prevention and crisis resources for you or your loved ones, and best practices for professionals.

TO WRITE LOVE ON HER ARMS:
twloha.com/find-help/
Find information about pregnancy centers, groups for dealing with substance abuse, mental illness support, and support groups if someone in your life has a serious illness. This is a great resource!

HUMAN TRAFFICKING: 1-888-373-7888
humantraffickinghotline.org/get-help

If you or someone you know needs help, call the National Human Trafficking Hotline toll-free hotline, 24 hours a day, 7 days a week to speak with a specially trained, anti-trafficking hotline advocate. Support is provided in more than 200 languages. They are there to listen and connect you with the help you need to stay safe.

24 HOUR PRAYER HOTLINE: 1-800-823-6053

Prayer Requests. 24 Hour Prayer Center.

24/7 CRISIS TEXT LINE: Text HOME to 741741

Crisis Text Line serves anyone, in any type of crisis, providing access to free, 24/7 support and information via a medium people already use and trust: text.

Chatnow.org

Free Christian help via online chatting with trained professionals (not counselors). They also offer help on specific topics on their website.